SPEEDBUMPS AND POTHOLES

For Linda

SPEEDBUMPS AND POTHOLES

Looking for Signs of God in the Everyday

NICK BAINES

SAINT ANDREW PRESS
Edinburgh

First published in 2004 by
SAINT ANDREW PRESS
121 George Street
Edinburgh EH2 4YN

Copyright © Nick Baines, 2004

ISBN 0 7152 0806 3

This book has been published with grant assistance from the
Drummond Trust, 3 Pitt Terrace, Stirling.

British Library Cataloguing in Publication Data
A catalogue record for this book is available from the British Library

Typeset by Waverley Typesetters, Galashiels
Printed and bound in the United Kingdom by Bell & Bain Ltd, Glasgow

CONTENTS

ACKNOWLEDGEMENTS

'Cry Of A Tiny Babe'
    Written by Bruce Cockburn
    © 1991 Golden Mountain Music Corp. (SOCAN)
    Used by permission

'All that you can't leave behind'
    Written by U2
    (Island CIDU212/548095–2) PolyGram International
    Music Publishing BV)

While every effort has been made to verify the accuracy of previously published quotations and to obtain permissions where appropriate, the publisher will be pleased to rectify any omission for future editions of this book.

FOREWORD

I first met Nick Baines when he presented an edition of Radio 2's *Pause for Thought*. It's a damned difficult 2½ minutes to pull off! Why? Well, having listened to ten years of them every morning at 6.15-ish, I feel qualified to underline just what a Pooh trap little innocent *Pause for Thought* can be. I've just calculated that I must have heard over 2,500 of them!

The speaker needs a solid argument, not a frothy cappuccino of a half-baked, non-thought through theme. The speaker needs a good voice, neither patronising nor unctuous. He or she should try to appeal to everybody listening, regardless of faith or circumstance. Are you of interest to Joe the Trucker who has driven through the night delivering the beer supplies to the Dog and Ferret and is now panting for his bed?

Are you holding the concentration of the young mum, up all night with her teething baby? Or, for that matter, the business person who's got an important presentation and speech at 11.00 a.m.? No, *P for T* is not easy, AND they don't pay very well either!

To ram home my point, you've also got to please cynics like Sarah Kennedy and colleagues such as 'Trevor Behind the Glass' in the studio, busy balancing levels and shoving wires into sockets, etc. We've heard good ones, mediocre ones and some that are downright awful. He cracked me up the other morning, setting up a pre-recorded *P for T*, when, on pre-hearing the tape, the first line went along the lines of 'Gilbert and

Sullivan wrote *The Gondoliers*, and it featured two gondoliers blah blah.' Trevor, sardonic as ever, muttered, 'wonder when the vicar will get round to asking if we knew that God was a gondolier?' Shades of Alan Bennett and his spoof sardine-can sermon!

The greatest compliment I can pay to Bishop Nick (far too youthful-looking for a Bishop) is to say he's always avoided these ecclesiastical Pooh traps. He speaks and writes from the heart. His message is intelligent, clear and well developed. He is funny if appropriate, but when there is a world tragedy, he's there like the clerical cavalry. Phew! A safe pair of vocal chords.

The last time he turned up live at Studio 1H (Broadcasting House), it was six in the morning and he was kitted out in trainers, slightly red-eyed, having delivered his daughter back to University, but quietly determined. He'd watched the first night of the latest Iraqi war unfold. No sleep, but was still absolutely excellent. What is my definition of dog collar 'excellent'? It's the spirit level isn't it? Do I feel better or worse after the statutory $2\frac{1}{2}$ minutes? Tick the Baines YES box! He roams around subjects. Nothing is sacred – moles, Hampton Court, loud music, Van Gogh, Angels, French cinemas, over-hobbied men. Nick Baines is a thoroughly modern churchman. His wife Linda calls him a 'model husband'. Ever curious, Nick looked up 'model' in the dictionary. It revealed, 'Model – a very small replica of the real thing'! Linda, you are very clever to have chosen a husband so wisely. If you ever tire of him, I've always fancied my own private chaplain!

Nick, congratulations on your book. On a blustery cold day, as I write this, you've worked your ecclesiastical magic and made me feel much sunnier. And that's a God-given gift.

Sarah Kennedy

INTRODUCTION

There are people who spend their lives looking for miracles, extraordinary signs that God is there and is not idle. For such people faith is reinforced by seeing God actively and obviously at work in the world. For other people, however, the miraculous seems remote. If God is there at all, he must be there in the midst of ordinary life and human experience. Although open to the former, I am most interested in the latter. Hence the curiosity behind these scripts.

Most of these reflections are based on ideas which found their way into broadcasts on local, regional or national radio. The challenge facing the broadcaster is to say something that teases the imagination and invites the hearer perhaps to see the world differently. This has to be done without preaching or patronising; it requires of the speaker that the language of the listener be understood.

Writing for the radio stimulates the imagination. Given that the ideas behind these reflections originate here, I am grateful to many people for giving me the opportunity to muse in this way in their media. For many years I worked with Sandra Herbert at BBC Radio Leicester. I also wrote material for commercial radio stations and owe a debt to Liz Jepson and Andrew Fewster. It has been a great and instructive pleasure to work with (mostly) Lucy Dichmont of The Unique Broadcasting Company in London and to intrude on the studio of Sarah Kennedy and her colleagues at Broadcasting House. These are wonderful people and I have learned from them all.

From time to time I have had to pass texts under the pedantic (but amusing) noses of my wife, Linda, and daughter, Melanie. I love them both and am grateful for their critical generosity . . . or were they just lying to keep me happy? (My sons, Richard and Andrew, were just critical . . .)

These reflections are not meant to offer the final word on the meaning of God, life, the universe and everything. Rather, they are reflections that arise from observation and ordinary, everyday experience. For me the most startling thing about being a Christian in the first place is the remarkable fact that God did not remain aloof from the world he made, but came and lived among us as one of us. The world of Jesus was material, full of water and wine, dirt and flesh. As a builder up north, he had to engage with economics and suffered the lot of those who refuse to keep God safe from politics. In his stories and pictures he pointed to the everyday experiences of his audience, but had the wisdom to let them use their own imagination and intellect to tease out what he was on about.

Where I live in South London we have speedbumps every few metres. They play havoc with car suspensions. We also 'enjoy' potholes the size of small oceans. These form part of the everyday experience of living, walking and driving in London. So even these might provide a fitting starting point for looking for signs of the God who has come among us and promised never to leave us. It might seem an odd place to start looking for the living God, but some would say a trough out the back of a house in a village in the Middle East was a stupid place to go looking for Emmanuel, God with us. Wouldn't they?

SEEING
DIFFERENTLY

REGRINDING THE LENS

I have to wear glasses for reading. I know this isn't the most embarrassing confession I could possibly make, but it is one of the most important. I have always prided myself on my perfect vision and could never understand what it must be like not to be able to see completely clearly. But a couple of years ago I discovered that I wasn't able to read without getting a headache and that I couldn't concentrate for long when doing close reading. So, now I have spectacles and I can see clearly, read extensively and focus precisely.

Now, that is as far as my interest in optometry goes. Once I couldn't see, but now I can. Hallelujah! *How* the lenses were produced and how they work is of little or no interest to me at all. I am not a scientist, and explanations of how light is refracted through lenses and perceived by my brain do not need to detain me for long. I don't understand and I am not interested. I guess an optician could explain it all to me and describe how the shape of the lens itself enables me to see, but I'm not sure I would actually understand any of it. All I know is that when I put my glasses on I can see what I am supposed to see.

It is said that all human beings have a lens *behind* the eyes – a metaphorical lens which is rarely or never taken out and subjected to critical analysis. This is the lens through which I see God, the world and myself. I don't often question what I see, but rather assume that what I see is how it is. And there is no more to be said on the matter. But, this lens is so important to the way I view life and death and joy and pain that I cannot leave it there, unexamined and untouchable.

In the New Testament there is a word which everybody knows and few understand: it is 'repentance'. You only have to say the word in the pub and people will assume it's about Christians wanting other people to grovel before God, lose their personality and become 'nice' people. But you might be surprised to learn that the Greek word 'metanoia' means literally 'a change of mind'. Or, as I might dare to represent it, it means having the lens behind the eyes reground so that when I look through it I see differently. For example, if I have a low opinion of my own value as a person, the reshaped lens might enable me better to see myself as God sees me: loved, valuable, full of potential. Instead of taking the world for granted, I might see that this creation is precious and in need of careful stewardship if it is not to be destroyed through selfish abuse. And if I picture God as a cruel policeman in the sky whose main pastime is trying to catch me out, I might need to see other images which speak of protective care, outrageous generosity and sacrificial love.

In other words, all human beings need from time to time to remove the lens behind their eyes, examine it carefully, allow it to be refashioned in order that they might see more clearly who they are, the world they are in and the God who cares for them. Seeing differently might change our lives, change our views and challenge our prejudices.

And that wouldn't be a bad start, would it?

BETWEEN TWO WORLDS

One of the interesting things about having teenage children – and there are many – is the discovery that they don't necessarily share the same taste in music as their parents. There are, of course, other interesting and challenging things about having teenage children . . . spots, for instance; or unimaginable quantities of deodorant in the air; or even, dare I say it, a frightening familiarity with computers, gadgets and anything electronic with buttons on it. But it's the music I'm sticking with for now.

Let's face it: a house with teenagers is a house without silence. If a room has a stereo in it, that stereo *must* be switched on. The fact that the telly is also on is a mere detail. That the said teenager has earphones from the personal minidisk player plugged in is clearly (but inexplicably) irrelevant to the need to create more musical noise. Wherever you go in the house, there is music and noise and more music and more noise.

I came home recently and was happily listening to a violin concerto in my study, quietly reflecting on the day. I didn't know anybody else was in the house . . . that is, until the counter-offensive began upstairs. I don't know which band it was (and, frankly, I have no interest in finding out), but it was in blatant conflict with my music. I felt cross, disturbed and confused. I couldn't decide whether to turn up the volume on the violin or give in and let the barrage from above win the day. But any uncertainty about my response could not disguise the certainty of my reaction: my temperature rose and my temper deteriorated.

However, once the matter was resolved and I once again found the time to think, the experience turned out not to be entirely negative. In fact, it almost seemed to symbolise something of life's struggle for many people in a complex world, illustrating what it is like for someone who wants to hold to certain values or beliefs in the face of a popular culture which thinks differently. For example, people who responded to the al-Qaeda terrorist attacks on New York in September 2001 with pleas for mercy and humility were sometimes ridiculed by the clamour for vengeance. Or, it can be uncomfortable to honour frail, elderly or less able people in a culture which worships beauty, reveres success and demands rights to self-fulfilment. It can be hard to work out which music to listen to and which to filter out. The competing rhythms and melodies do not harmonise, but merely threaten to confuse and challenge the audience. It's a bit like living between two worlds, not always being sure which one is the more substantial. How do you choose what to think or how to live? Which tune do you listen to amid the cacophony in the air?

I guess that's really what faith is all about: living *with* the contradictions and competing rhythms of real life . . . while straining to hang onto one melody line despite the unharmonious clashes. That's the reality of faithful living in a confusing world. It is the constant struggle for anyone who does not want to be blown about by any spirit of the age, swayed by any siren voice or seductive melody, but who wants to hear the truth and live aright. And it proves the difficulty of, as Jesus once put it, 'being in the world, but not of it'.

Oh . . . and, if you are interested, I shut the door and turned up the volume of the violin concerto!

MOLES AND OTHER QUESTIONS

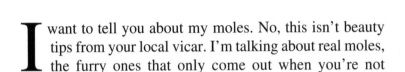

I want to tell you about my moles. No, this isn't beauty tips from your local vicar. I'm talking about real moles, the furry ones that only come out when you're not looking.

When I lived with my family in a Leicestershire vicarage, we had a huge garden. It had big old trees, a river running through it and far too much grass for cutting. It backed on to a field in which the farmer grazed his cows. Ducks used to climb up out of the river and cuddle the ducklings on the lawn in the sunshine. It was a beautiful place to live and every day revealed something new in nature's rich menu of experiences and views.

I recall one day – my day off – when I thought I'd get to grips with the garden. I have to admit that this was not my favourite pastime – I do not have green fingers – but in winter I couldn't get away with claiming hay fever as an excuse for not doing it. When I got outside I got a terrible shock. The grass, which my wife had been carefully growing and mowing for years, was wrecked. It looked as if mini-volcanoes had erupted everywhere. But whereas moles usually seem to run in a line, pushing up the soil at intervals, this one must have been drunk. There were holes everywhere – in circles in one area. And it must have been the stupidest mole in Leicestershire because in one place it had even tried to come up under a tree trunk.

I hate moles, but I have a sneaking admiration for what they do. The surface may look lovely, the garden may appear serene; but under it all there's something burrowing around and making an embarrassing mess. And just when you think you've got the little beasts cornered, they disappear, lie low for a couple of days, then re-emerge with an ironic, mocking push of the soil. Even the cat eventually gave up trying to get this one.

One of my boyhood heroes had a molish outlook on life. John Lennon wrote a great song which had the refrain, 'But one thing you can't hide is when you're crippled inside'. He was one of those who questioned the accepted account of why the world was the way it was. He dared to challenge the superficial and the safe by digging away underneath the surface of things and exposing the truth as he saw it. He may not have always been right, but he was right to try. He was a mole-man.

It seems to me that mole-people dig around at what lies under the surface. They are never satisfied with nice appearances when what lies underneath is more painful or ugly. They keep asking the questions others would rather ignore. Just when you think you've got all the answers they pop up with the question which makes you have to start all over again. They're more interested in truth and reality than convenience or comfort.

Jesus was a mole-man like this. He had a habit of being awkward, of disturbing the comfortable and comforting the disturbed:

- Are people *really* born to shop, simply to be consumers of things?

- Is any footballer really worth tens of millions of pounds? Or is he worth exactly the same as you and me and the vulnerable refugees of this world's conflicts?

- Is profit really more important than people's lives when it comes to exporting arms to shadowy foreign regimes?

- Why do we think that just because we *can* do human cloning, we *should* do it?

- Is the market really free? And who pays the price for the freedom of some?

I realise Jesus wouldn't have got his diploma from the British School of Tact and Diplomacy, but he went as far as calling the religious leaders of his day 'tarted up tombs'. They might have been nice and decorous on the outside, but inside they were full of rottenness and foul smells. I have a vague suspicion that those on the receiving end didn't exactly warm to this judgement.

The truth can often be difficult to hear – especially by those who are convinced of their own rightness.

SPEEDBUMPS AND POTHOLES

Whatever resources Yuri Gagarin took with him when he became the first human being to fly into space, he certainly did not go without a bag full of prejudices. On his return (which was not very long after his departure) he boldly and ironically proclaimed that he had not encountered God 'up there' where some people think heaven is to be found. Well, give the man a medal for stating the blindingly obvious.

Gagarin was not, perhaps, the most subtle of thinkers when it came to the question of God's existence or absence. Thousands of years of human experience and spiritual longings were not to be discounted by the not-very-profound observation of an astronaut who thought that God could be irrefutably debunked in such an easy way. It is a bit like looking in the manger at Christmas and singing 'no crying he makes' – no wonder people think Jesus was not real if fantasy is the starting point.

A similar experience is common when people suffer a crisis or bereavement. They cry out for God to intervene from 'out there' and get angry when he appears not to do so. And yet the heart of Christian faith is that God is to be found not 'out there', remote from human experience and the lot of the world, but 'right here' where we live out our lives. 'Immanuel' means 'God with us', right here where the pain and joy are most acute, right here where the answers to human dilemmas do not always come easily to us.

Look at this another way. When Jesus walked this earth he didn't speak of God in merely conceptual terms. Rather, when he addressed a wide range of people of his time he used images, metaphors, stories and language to which his various audiences could relate. In one sense, he brought God 'down to earth' and rooted him in the here and now. Many of the stories he told (parables) relate to the growing of his kingdom (his rule) now, in this time and space, with these people.

An Asian theologian called Kosuke Koyama once wrote a book called *Water Buffalo Theology*. There aren't any water buffalo in South London where I live (although nothing would surprise me any more), but there are other features of life which serve a similar purpose. I can look around at what I see every day and see signs of God, pointers to his presence, or just images which spark my thinking about the reality of life with God. Outside my house, for example, is a pothole which will soon be reclassified as a deep-shaft mine. Just up the road are a series of speedbumps which the Council hopes will slow down the traffic (rather than just keep replacement suspension manufacturers in business).

Recently I watched a car speed up the road, hit the pothole with a bang, then roar off until it screeched almost to a halt in front of the speedbump. The driver seemed frustrated. But if he drove wisely, taking note of the realities outside his metal framework, he would have proceeded without delay and more consistently. Watching this made me reflect that I face similar choices in life: I don't like the fact that the world and being human throws up all sorts of unwelcome obstacles, or that sometimes it seems as if the road has just fallen away beneath my wheels. But if I just slow down and pay attention to the world around me, I might well discover that the potholes and speedbumps serve many purposes – not least that I might have to slow down if I am to notice the obstacles before me.

That said, however, I can still think of other pictures of God's presence which would be recognised if the Council did the sensible thing and filled the pothole.

COWS AND CURIOSITY

———————— ❖ ————————

During the aeons of human history and civilisation wise men and women have revealed some power-ful truths about the world – truths which have sub-sequently been handed down from generation to generation, enabling people to live more humanely, more discerningly. Well, now it is my turn. So, prepare to absorb something that is mind-blowingly important and absolutely true: *You can lead a cow upstairs, but you can't lead a cow down-stairs.*

Now then . . . that'll change your life, won't it!? Well, it might do if you're a farmer with a block of flats for a cowshed. I actually heard that little bit of wisdom about cattle on the car radio while trying to negotiate the Wandsworth one-way system in London – in my view, a task somewhat harder than getting a cow to walk downstairs.

Getting to London in the first place was an interesting experience. The M1 isn't the most exciting road in the world. However, one of the landmarks I noticed was a bridge onto which someone has painted in large white letters: *Give me inspiration!* I sympathised with the sentiment. Whoever decided the bridge needed that particular graffiti had obviously done the same journey I was doing.

Well, believe it or not, these two things – cows and the plea for inspiration – hold together in a rather peculiar but interesting way. The trivia industry (and there are hundreds of sites on the Internet devoted simply to trivial knowledge and useless information) is born of our human curiosity about the world and the way it works. Weird facts of life such as cows' fear of descent tickle our imagination and reinforce for us the hope that life is more complex and colourful than the daily routine might suggest. And, contrary to popular conviction, inspiration doesn't simply invade a sterile mind from nowhere; rather, it emerges from a mind that is always curious, constantly questioning the world, observing, looking, seeing, wondering.

The ancient writers of the Bible made the bold claim that we human beings are made in the image of God. This seems to me to be right. For the world that God has created is one which evokes curiosity at every turn, offering the possibility of inspired thinking and imagining. It's a world of music and poetry and pictures and untamed, surprising beauty. And we are a people whose imaginations are teased and constantly provoked by a God who, in the person of Jesus of Nazareth, invites us to look at the world and ourselves through different eyes or lenses. Ordinary people followed him because he fired their hearts and inspired their imaginations about what *might* be. He warned adults that they would miss the point about God if they didn't become like children – that is, infinitely curious and unwilling to be fobbed off with the simplistic.

As for me, I want my curiosity to grow and my questioning of the world to develop. I'll plead for inspiration and enjoy all sorts of trivia which put colour into a complex life. And, because I got carried away by these musings and didn't listen to the rest of the radio programme, I'll just have to continue to wonder *why* a cow cannot be led downstairs.

FLOWERS IN THE DESERT

My friends will tell you that flowers are *not* my thing. I'm not too good on nature generally, but flowers leave me stumped. When horticultural knowledge was granted to humanity, I was weeded out of the queue. Maybe it's because I get terrible hay fever and my ignorance is a sort of primal defence mechanism designed to prevent me from even getting interested in getting close to petals and sepals (. . . whatever they are). Anyway, whatever the reasons, I'm not good at plants.

When I was studying at a theological college in Bristol in the mid-1980s, I spent Friday afternoons on the college gardening team. I remember being asked to weed the old rose garden in front of the main building. I spent a happy two hours pulling up the huge amount of scrawny green things only then to be told that I had just uprooted all the plants which had been painstakingly planted the previous week. It's not a happy record and I am not exaggerating. For twenty years I have bought my wife carnations, only recently to find out that she hates them, but didn't like to hurt my feelings. And to think that for all these years I could have got her dandelions instead!

I'm just not very good when it comes to flora and, for that matter, fauna.

But there is one thing I do know: some flowers grow only in particular environments. This fact was brought home to me in a story told by a friend of mine. A missionary had returned from an arid and tough part of Africa to attend a Christian conference in the UK. He was depressed and flat and the last thing he wanted to do was attend a gathering such as this one. Then a speaker got up to the rostrum and began his address as follows:

> There are some flowers that only grow in the desert. If you are in the desert there is no point looking for flowers that only grow in the fertile places: you will be perpetually disappointed. But look for the unique flowers that grow only in the desert in which you find yourself and you will be richly rewarded.

My friend was stopped in his cynicism. It was no use constantly wishing that life could be better or easier. He was in a desert and he could either become increasingly frustrated at not being somewhere else, or he could try looking at the world differently. He chose the latter and returned to Africa transformed. His circumstances had not changed. But he had been changed within them.

I think it is like this with God. There are some experiences of God and lessons about him that cannot take place where all is fine with life. It is sometimes when we are stripped of all the securities and trappings of a comfortable life that we meet God in the barren place where he simply walks slowly with us.

So, even though the idea might seem a little twee, there might be enormous value in changing the lens through which I look at my circumstances of life. After all, this is primarily what prayer is about: changing me within my circumstances, not exempting me from them. It's about coming to see the world and my situation through God's eyes and, therefore, responding to them differently.

So, as the seasons continue their cycle, I will be looking for those things I might otherwise miss. I will enjoy the winter for what it is, not for what it isn't. And I will consider once again how looking outside of myself can help me reflect on how I look within.

FAITH IN OBLIVION

I have looked into the empty, terrifying darkness of the Black Hole. I have stared Nemesis in the face, felt my heart pounding in my chest. I have confronted Oblivion and survived. I have been to Alton Towers . . . and I am very, very scared.

Well, not that scared! I'll tell you what Oblivion is like in a minute. But first let me explain what happens on Nemesis. You queue for an hour during which time you question your sanity. When your time comes, you sit in your seat and pull the harness down over your chest. The harness is clipped onto a seat belt. The floor disappears beneath you. You are pulled up a steep slope until, high above the queueing crowds, you are thrown down, around, upside-down, to the left and to the right. You end up, thirty seconds later, staggering out of your seat and laughing through the tears. It is brilliant.

However, when I get into the seat I keep pulling on the harness. I want to make sure it will hold me when I'm being thrown around. There is always an element of doubt in my mind, but I am too proud to chicken out at the last moment. I ultimately trust the engineers, the safety people and the fact that thousands of other people have done this ride without falling off.

That is faith.

When people tell me they have faith in God (or anything else for that matter), I look at their life to see if they are telling me the truth. It is not enough to believe that God is trustworthy or reliable. It is not enough to *think* I believe something. The reality of faith is seen when I commit my life to it. I may say I believe in a God who loves me, who forgives me when I fall and sets me free. But if I don't live my life in the truth of that belief, I am a hypocrite. If I despise myself and hate my fellows, this demonstrates that my 'belief' in this God is simply wishful thinking or romantic sentimentality. Faith means action. If God forgives me, I must be gracious in forgiving others who sin against me.

Or, if I believe that God is the creator and sustainer of the universe and that, as the Old Testament poet put it, 'The earth is the Lord's and everything in it', but live as if the world can be exploited without regard for the well-being of the earth and all its people, then I am kidding myself (though probably not others). The reality is simply that I believe the world is mine to do what I like with and God is as much a fantasy as Father Christmas and Cinderella's fairy godmother.

Now, back to Oblivion. With this one you get in a carriage, ride up high, then hang over a vertical drop before plunging into the void and screaming blue murder. No faith is needed to stand on the ground in Alton Towers looking up at Oblivion and proclaiming, 'I believe I would be safe to go on that.' You have to get on it and go over the edge before I'll believe you. (I chickened out.)

LOOKING THROUGH OTHER EYES

AN USHERETTE IN PARIS

Never go to the cinema in France without taking lots of spare cash with you. Many years ago, while working in Paris, I went with some friends to see a Dustin Hoffman film at a cinema on the Boulevard St Michel. All eleven of us were broke and had just shared a ham sandwich as our evening meal. Between us we could just about muster the money to get us all in. The delightful usherette was very friendly. She smiled with the persistence of an international athlete and insisted on shaking hands with each one of us. The preliminaries over, she then led us into an empty cinema and showed us to an equally empty row of seats. We could have sat anywhere. But she insisted on showing us, with her impressive little torch, to our places. We smiled, thanked her repeatedly and sat down. She was clearly and excessively pleased to see us.

Well, I hear you say, isn't that heart-warming and a good omen for Franco-British relations? Maybe it is, but a slight problem arose when she didn't go away. And it seemed that nothing could persuade her to leave us alone. She seemed so pleased to see me, I was beginning to wonder when she was going to propose marriage. Not for the first time I had drawn the short straw in the positioning lottery of life and was sitting on the end of the row, right next to the aisle still occupied by the lovely usherette. She flashed her eyes, smiled coquettishly and hovered expectantly. I was sure she had fallen in love with me and I basked in the romance for what seemed like . . . seconds. Then reality struck with depressing clarity: she was waiting for a tip.

I nudged my neighbour and asked if he had any money for the tip. He had none, but he kindly nudged his neighbour with the same request. And so it went on, all the way up the line and all the way back down again. No one had a centime. And I had no idea how to break the news to the usherette, who must have thought it was her lucky day when she saw eleven of us walk in. I shrugged my shoulders and muttered that we didn't have anything to give her. She became enraged, started calling me obscene names (most of which I understood), and then spent the whole film standing to one side and shining her torch in my eyes. It was a hopeless film anyway!

What I hadn't realised, of course, is that she received no wage for her work. She lived off the tips. Hence her anger and disappointment. It was days later before I had this explained to me and, quite naturally, I felt very embarrassed. Our tips might have been her meal for that night and once I could see the situation through her eyes it took on a completely different significance. Seeing it this way changed me and my perception. I have never forgotten it and still wish I could find her to apologise for our ignorance. I should have learned how things are done in Paris and seen the encounter through her eyes.

It seems to me that this is precisely what Jesus of Nazareth was trying to do: get people to see through different eyes. He wanted them to open themselves to the possibility that there is more to life and to God than their experiences or assumptions hitherto had led them to believe. Yes, this would challenge their prejudices and confound simple self-justification. Yes, it would open their eyes to new obligations and make them see their own actions differently. And yes, there would be a cost.

But, just as in my meeting with the usherette in Paris, it might just change the world for someone, and not only me.

ALARM CLOCKS AND WAKE-UP CALLS

When God gave out the ability to wake up bright and fresh in the morning, my brother and I weren't even at the back of the queue: we'd overslept.

So why, you might ask, did my brother go for a job in the Post Office? Being a postman means getting up at a time which might be described as BC (before consciousness). Well, what he did, in fact, was get a huge brass alarm clock and cover it with pan lids and things. If he didn't get to it before it rang, he got whacked by falling metal and loud noises. Unfortunately, because I shared a room with him, he wasn't the only one to get woken by the sound of the end of the world.

I was reminded of this during a trip to Indonesia several years ago. I had never been to Asia before and knew that the whole experience would be new to me. After the longest flights in history I arrived at my friends' house in Jakarta around 9 o'clock in the evening and soon went to bed. Despite my tiredness, I woke unexpectedly at 4.30 a.m. I felt disorientated and confused, unsure of where I was and what was going on. I could hear a loud voice moaning through the window of my room. My first conscious thought was: 'Oh no, they warned me not to come to Indonesia during the current violence.' I eventually realised that what I was hearing was the muezzin at the local mosque calling the faithful Moslems to prayer. 'Sleep', he wailed, 'is not as important as coming to pray to almighty God.' 'Good idea', I thought, 'but does it have to be so early?'

During the five weeks I was in Jakarta I managed to turn what, frankly, I had thought would be an irritant, specially designed to make waking up uncomfortable, into a significant part of the day. That muezzin was challenging not only his faithful Moslem congregation but also me to get my priorities right. I live a fairly fast and busy life, days and evenings filled with people and activity. It is easy to mistake the urgent for the important. It is a simple matter to busy myself to distraction. But if my life is to be ordered and I am to be at peace, I must learn to be quiet, to make time for reflection and prayer, to make a priority of stopping the world – even for a few minutes – to listen and look.

The psalmist wrote: 'Be still and know that I am God.' I guess he had realised that frenetic activity is the enemy of knowing God and of peaceful living. The importance of getting the perspective right and the priorities clear is easily ignored amid the demands of contemporary living in the Western world. And I still find it funny that it took a muezzin eight thousand miles away to remind me that I must make space for being still with God each day. But I still wish it didn't have to be at 4.30 a.m.

RUBBER TIME

During my visit to Indonesia I stayed with friends at their home in Jakarta. Every day brought new experiences, some fascinating, others bizarre. Never before had I been in a country or culture where I didn't know the language and felt so very vulnerable. I was constantly looking through new eyes, observing new sights and trying to make some sense out of the whole thing. One day I tried to do something in private that I was too ashamed to try in public. I would have felt both embarrassed and conspicuous. I tried to squat with my bottom resting just above my heels. I wanted to see for how long I could sit there in that position.

Now, I accept that this is probably all the evidence you need to prove that I had too much time on my hands or that I should just get out a bit more. My kids would simply have advised me to 'get a life'. But this squatting experiment was not just the product of idleness. It was more a scientific inquiry into the nature of time. It was a serious – though nonetheless embarrassing – exercise, but I recognise that further explanation is now necessary.

One of the first things to hit your consciousness when you arrive in Jakarta is the sheer number of men who appear to just sit around. Day after day they just sit there, often in the same spot, watching the world go by. And the amazing thing is that they often don't sit *on* anything. They just squat down on their heels and stay there. They all seem to have a very equable temperament and simply sit and watch life pass them by. Sometimes they are waiting for a bus or for the rain to stop. Sometimes they are talking or attending to a stall at the side of the road, waiting for custom. But, clearly, sometimes they are simply sitting there. Isn't it a waste of time, time they could be using more productively?

Before coming out to Indonesia I was warned about the concept of 'rubber time'. Basically, this means what it seems: time is flexible. When I attend a meeting in England I expect it to begin at the appointed time and finish at the appointed time. If a wedding is booked for 12 noon, I expect the bride to arrive in good time so that the service can begin on time and all the other arrangements follow accordingly. And maybe the clue to the difference lies here: I speak of being 'on time', whereas rubber time has to do with being 'in time'. In Indonesia the event begins when the people are gathered. It is the presence of the people that dictates the event, not vice versa. Consequently, having been attending to possibly unexpected guests is more than adequate excuse for arriving late at or even missing a previously arranged event.

So, maybe the men who squat on their heels for hours on end are not wasting their time after all, but living in it, experiencing it. Instead of being dictated to by events, diaries and timetables, they live in the time they have and not on it. Perhaps in having the time or temperament to reflect and watch the world go by, they are living more deeply than I am.

Naturally I realise that this is hopelessly romantic. Of course 'rubber time' and its inherent potential for lack of discipline is infuriating and is perhaps an indication of why the economy was in a catastrophic mess. But that shouldn't stop me from asking whether its ranking of people above business doesn't have something to say to frenetic, time-obsessed Westerners. Perhaps it might make me reflect also on why it is so difficult to wait *for* and wait *on* God in a culture which is enslaved to the demands of instant satisfaction. Maybe I should stop in more and thereby get a life – a life of depth, not just speedy superficiality.

Incidentally, I lasted only forty seconds in the squat position before my knees started cracking and my ankles ached.

HIGH-RISE BUILDINGS

I love looking at buildings. I wouldn't know where to begin to build one, but I love looking at them. For many of us the sheer familiarity of the environment we live in – especially in cities – can easily blind us to the richness of the architecture which frames our every view. In London, where I live, there are some marvellous buildings, from ancient to modern, but they are easily missed as you push through the crowds and the traffic to get to your destination. I have to keep reminding myself to look up every now and then.

That's why it can be so good to go abroad. You can't help but be more sensitive to what is around you, especially when it is a place you have never encountered before. During my visit to Indonesia, I was amazed at the sheer design creativity and imagination of many of the high-rise buildings in Jakarta, the capital city. They are the sort of buildings you can sit and look at for hours without getting bored. In fact, you get hours to do just that while sitting in endless traffic jams unable to move.

The house I was staying in was a beautiful two-storey building with marble floors, carved wooden fittings, a large swimming pool and – oh mercy – banana trees. It looked wonderful . . . until I saw some cracks in the floor and walls. I was told that the house had begun to move after several years of little rain followed by that year's monsoon. Unfortunately, when some of the cracking marble stones were raised for inspection, it was discovered that there were no foundations.

Now I couldn't help wondering that if the *houses* are like this, what about the high-rise towers in the city centre? Are they *also* all image and no substance? Once you know there is nothing underneath the walls that surround you, it is remarkable how quickly you begin to feel insecure. A beautiful appearance will mean nothing if the earth moves and there are no foundations to take the strain.

It's funny how buildings can become symbols of what is happening in a culture at a particular time. The great sky-scrapers which dominate the Asian horizon are relics of yesterday's economic boom. They brag and boast of money and power. Reflective blue and black glass circular towers rise up reflecting the sky and its infinite possibilities. Green-peaked, pink-bricked, sleek edifices reach upwards, standing four-square on solid ground. Conceived and built during the 1980s and 1990s they exude confidence, boldness, playful adventure.

But many dozens of these buildings are now the empty shells of bankrupt banks. Built on confidence and illusion during the boom years, now these towers look naked and exposed to the real world, evidence of what can happen when confidence is placed in systems which are ill founded and customs which are frequently corrupt. It confronts the tourist as well as the native with the inescapable truth that image will ultimately not hide reality: the truth will out, regardless of how blind we wish to remain.

This has echoes of a story Jesus told about a wise man who built a house on rock and a foolish man who, in his rush to get it all now, built on a dodgy foundation, with ultimately disastrous consequences. Foundations are neither sexy nor visible. But they matter more than what stands upon them. Or, as John Lennon put it, 'One thing you can't hide is when you're crippled inside'.

In a world in which image is everything, I think we should rebel with freedom and joy. We should learn to deal only with substance and reality . . . and check out our foundations regularly. Start digging now!

12

LIGHT AT THE END OF THE TUNNEL

A visit to Israel–Palestine can be a depressing experience. The agonies inflicted by 'victims' on all sides
of the conflict are unbearable to those who suffer.
You only have to sit in the company of a Palestinian family
whose sons have been humiliated by Israeli soldiers, or hear
the passionate cries of a Jewish mother whose daughter got
on a school bus one morning, but never got off it again, to
feel that the agonising suffering is bound to continue. But
then you meet one of those people who make you feel you
are in the presence of someone remarkable. Recently, on a
trip to the Middle East, I met someone whose courage was
clear: it was Rabbi Michael Melchior, the then Deputy
Foreign Minister of Israel.

At a meeting in his Jerusalem office with a group of
Christian leaders he gave a passionate and very humane
analysis of the tragedy that is contemporary Israel. I didn't
have to agree with what he was saying, but was struck by
some of the language he used. For example, speaking of the
shockingly painful situation for both Palestinian Moslems
and Israeli Jews, he said this of attempts to broker some sort
of just peace: 'If there isn't light at the end of the tunnel, it
isn't because the light isn't there, it's because the tunnel isn't
straight.'

This evocative statement fired my own imagination
immediately. There is always a temptation, when things are

going badly and there seems to be no hope, to think that the light is not there, that the darkness is all there is. The future closes in and everything seems hopeless. I know from my experience of the thousands of people I have met in my life as a vicar that this experience is not rare. History is littered with the stories of people who have suffered unimaginably and innocently, finding their understanding of life's meaning and purpose seriously challenged.

But it seems important to recognise that when the future looks too difficult and there seems to be no light at the end of the tunnel, it might be because the tunnel itself is just not straight. And, furthermore, we have to learn to develop a longer-term view, thus rejecting the pressure to live only in the instant.

The experience of people in the Bible demonstrates this at every turn: that it is often where God appears to be absent and the darkness impenetrable that God is most powerfully present. Whether it be the people of Israel waiting for their exile to end or the disciples of Jesus finding their world falling apart on Crucifixion Friday, but not knowing that Resurrection Sunday lies ahead, people had to learn to wait and trust.

An anonymous Jew, hiding from the Gestapo in the German city of Cologne in 1942, scrawled on the wall of a cellar:

> I believe in the sun though it is late in rising.
> I believe in love though it is absent.
> I believe in God though he is silent.

Or, as the Gospel of John puts it: 'The light has shone in the darkness, and the darkness shall never overcome it.'

13

THE DIGNITY OF DIFFERENCE

I guess it's one of the facts of modern life that if you enjoy stroking the pussy cat of fame and publicity, you might also end up being bitten by it when it has had enough of your attentions. And although some people love causing controversy, others hate it, but have to endure it. Well, one public figure famously got into trouble with his own community by writing a book called *The Dignity of Difference*. Chief Rabbi, Dr Jonathan Sacks, later agreed to clarify what he meant in what some regarded as sensitive or contentious passages of the book.

But it was the title of his book (rather than its content) that has grabbed my attention. In fact, this was the phrase that came to mind on a Friday evening in Jerusalem several years ago when I went with a group of English Christian leaders to the Western Wall for the Jewish Sabbath. It was a new and bewildering experience for me. As more and more people arrived down by the ancient Temple walls the scene appeared to become increasingly chaotic. To the uneducated eye it looked like hundreds of men were arguing, praying, dancing, or apparently just chatting. They wore different styles of clothing, each one identifying the man as a member of a particular Jewish culture or group.

And this was precisely the point: lots of different types of Jews were gathering for worship in the same place. Once a group of ten had formed, they could begin their service. But there was no leader at the front telling people to stand for the next hymn or to kneel for prayer. Instead, these groups of people simply did the service when they were ready and in the way that suited them. Modern liberal Jews could be seen dancing and singing with their Orthodox brothers; others were praying quietly, nodding backwards and forwards, whispering the words of their liturgy. In other words, there wasn't simply a single acceptable form of worship or culture. People could worship quietly or loudly, static or dancing wildly, with singing or silence. But however you chose to do it, it was the same service and your way was acceptable. And, what's more, it all happened in the same place and space.

I think monochrome uniformity is the enemy of life, of colour and joy. Surely, where God is, and where people of all sorts come to worship, there must be life and joy and the dignity of difference – people being able to be themselves and worship in their way. The repeated message of the Bible is that God wants openness, integrity and honesty of heart and mind. And that means respecting differences of style, taste, culture and personality. Raising my hands and dancing is no more legitimate or 'holy' in God's eyes than kneeling in silence with my head bowed.

Following this experience all I can say is that Christian leaders like me have a lot to learn from the Jews of Jerusalem. But, in case you're nosey, on that particular evening I was the strong, silent type – my dancing would have brought worship to a halt and laughter to the lips of the greatest saint.

OUTSIDE THE BOX

A famous politician once verbally assassinated an opponent by saying that 'greater love has no man than this, that he lay down his friends for his life'. Of course, this is a parody of what Jesus said to his disciples prior to his own death, but it is also probably an accurate account of how many people actually behave. It can take enormous courage to reject this political maxim and embrace the value system behind Jesus' statement. I've got a story that might just illustrate this.

In the Middle East there are politicians who are finally admitting that they have run dry of ideas and short of hope. How, then, can there be a way forward in a peace process that becomes more derelict every time a Palestinian teenager blows himself up on a bus or an Israeli soldier shoots an unarmed civilian? It seems that when one party is hurt, the only response can be to hurt the one who caused this pain in the first place. And this leads to a cycle of unending violence and hatred which seems to allow for no resolution. Everyone becomes a victim and, so, nobody has to take responsibility for initiating a solution and paying the price of healing.

But what has not been widely reported is the work of a small group of religious leaders, led by the Archbishop of Canterbury. The key player in what is called 'The Alexandria Process' is an Anglican priest called Canon Andrew White who is Director of the Centre for International Reconciliation at Coventry Cathedral. This process has brought together Jewish rabbis, Moslem sheikhs and Christian patriarchs in a common conversation about reconciliation where there are no cheap solutions to conflict and no easy peace – especially if peace is simply seen as the absence of conflict. These brave people are able to embrace each other as brothers simply because they have been given a safe space outside of the political arena in which they can be human. Here they can use a different language and start from a common humanity.

The political discourse is dominated by the defence and propagation of rights. Add into this the ingredients of religious faith, ethnic identity and tribal history and you find political leaders viewing religion as the cause of the problem rather than the source of a solution. It seems that only when the political discourse becomes redundant does religion get a look in – and only then do words such as 'forgiveness' and 'reconciliation' gain a real currency.

Clearly, the work of Andrew White and his colleagues has opened up the possibility of a new hope and a new way of relating. Politicians who find themselves trapped in the cycle of rights and revenge are offered a safe place, a third way, a new language for hope. And, to return to where we began, it is rooted in the call of the carpenter from Nazareth who was willing to lay down his life for his friends rather than continue to spill the blood of somebody else's children.

THOUGHTS
ON THE WAY

MOVING ON

A pparently one of the most stressful things you can do in life is to move house. A couple of years ago, while most people were coming towards the end of their summer holidays, my mind was anything but relaxed. The travelling had come to an end, the tan was beginning to fade, and the autumn loomed. Children were preparing to return to school, businesses were gearing up for the end of the summer lull and the routine of life – uninterrupted by other people's holidays – would soon be resumed.

Well, not in our house it wouldn't! We had recently moved from a village in Leicestershire to the urban village of Streatham in South London. For us a new journey was beginning. And the truth that 'life never stands still' was, once again, being ruthlessly reaffirmed. Having been uprooted from all that had become so familiar for nearly a decade, we now had to make a new life in a new place with new people, new challenges and new opportunities.

Now I would be lying if I said that all this didn't cause us some trepidation as a family. The unknown future always beckons with both promise and threat. But this idea of life as a journey can be helpful at a time of great upheaval and change.

Our moving from Leicestershire meant *leaving some things behind*. The removals firm packed up our belongings, but left the bricks and mortar and soil and grass. We couldn't take everything into our new life in London. Even some of what in the past had made life good or bad had to be consigned to history. But to do this confronted us with serious questions about what really matters, how lightly we can travel through life, where the balance comes between the value of things and the value of relationships.

This was the experience of many characters in the Bible. Their calling wasn't always either welcome or comfortable. Abram was called to leave his home and embark on a journey to he knew not where. Jesus called Peter and other working men and women to walk with him, leaving behind the familiar things that gave life shape and meaning. Indeed, only in this way could they be free to embrace the new gifts that lay ahead. The only promise or guarantee they were given was that God would never abandon them, that whatever lay ahead he would be with them to the end.

But you don't have to move house or city to address these questions. The call of God has always been, and I guess always will be, for us to let go of some of our experiences, memories or regrets – even comfortable things – in order to move on to new experiences and understandings of the world, ourselves and God. We travel with promise and hope. And each journey will always be utterly unique.

Mind you, having begun to experience London traffic, I have a feeling some further reflections on journeys may follow.

TRAVELLING LIGHT

My kids are sick of my taste in music. OK, I'm now officially a fogey in their estimation. Every single tape in my car is by the same musician. I have his CDs playing in the house most of the time. I read his lyrics as I would read a poetry book and I listen over and over to his incredible guitar playing. I'm a Bruce Cockburn fan and I am proud of it!

I have to be very careful, though, when I make the next confession. If my kids hear this, they'll probably divorce me, so I'll write it quietly: twenty years ago I was greatly influenced by a Cliff Richard song. Yes, I know it's embarrassing, but it happens to be true. Actually it was only one track and it was a re-record of a song he'd already done years before that. The song is 'Travelling Light'. I can't even remember what it was about, but the title made an impression on me and my wife.

Linda and I had just got married and we were buying a small house and expecting our first child. I was a professional linguist and she was a nurse. We had absolutely no money. Considering the future and what we thought we should do with our lives, we tackled the question of values and possessions. When you've got very little it's dead easy to be pious about possessions. But we made a commitment then which we still try to hold to now, nearly twenty years later. That is, to travel light; never to be so rooted in *things* that we wouldn't be able to let them go. So that Cliff Richard song kept haunting us: 'Travelling Light.'

As the Old Testament writer said, there is a time for keeping and a time for throwing away. Maybe the time for throwing away comes when we are too attached to something which takes on too much importance in our lives – perhaps something we value above people.

Jesus said that it is easier to get a Rolls Royce through a revolving door than it is for a rich man to enter the kingdom of heaven . . . or something to that effect, anyway. Perhaps the people of his day were no different from us, perhaps they just had different attachments. But our consumer society can easily seduce us and skew our values and relationships. Are we really born to shop? Descartes said, 'Cogito ergo sum' (I think, therefore I am), but we say 'Tesco ergo sum' (I shop, therefore I am). There is something worrying about a society that has learned how to buy, but forgotten how to play. And there is something profoundly disturbing about a culture which builds shopping cathedrals and then wonders why everything smells of plastic.

I think I'll try to stick with travelling light and keeping things in perspective. Despite Cliff Richard. And please don't tell my children.

17

PILGRIM FATHERS

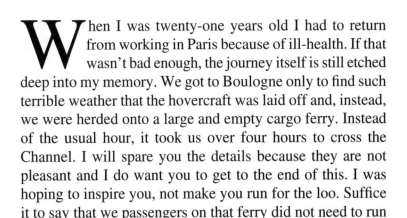

When I was twenty-one years old I had to return from working in Paris because of ill-health. If that wasn't bad enough, the journey itself is still etched deep into my memory. We got to Boulogne only to find such terrible weather that the hovercraft was laid off and, instead, we were herded onto a large and empty cargo ferry. Instead of the usual hour, it took us over four hours to cross the Channel. I will spare you the details because they are not pleasant and I do want you to get to the end of this. I was hoping to inspire you, not make you run for the loo. Suffice it to say that we passengers on that ferry did not need to run for the loo – it seemed to keep running to us! OK – enough said! You've got the idea . . .

When I had come out of hospital and recovered enough to travel, I went to visit my then fiancée (now my wife) who lived on the Wirral. I went from my home in Liverpool to the Pier Head and got on the Mersey Ferry. The river was still, the sun shone, and all was well with the world. Almost. You see, as soon as I got on the boat and sat on the top deck, I became aware of its subtle movement, the gentle throbbing of the engines. And suddenly, involuntarily, the experience of that Channel crossing flooded back into my consciousness. I only just made it to Birkenhead.

I was reminded of this when I read recently about the departure of the Pilgrim Fathers from Plymouth as they headed for the New World. They knew what they were leaving behind, but had little idea of what awaited them across the enormous ocean. Their ship was relatively small and insecure; but they set off anyway because they had a vision of a different way of living in a different sort of country. I cannot bear to think about what the journey must have been like. I just know I couldn't have done it.

What impresses me about the Pilgrims is simply this: they had a vision of a different world. They were prepared to leave a familiar world behind them in order to pursue this vision. It cost them everything, but still they cast the anchor and sailed away. The threat of the unknown did not deter them from leaving; the promise of the unknown possibilities enticed them to risk everything. Lack of certainty about the journey itself did not prevent them embarking and hoisting their sails.

It comes as no surprise then that this forms a strong picture of what God has always called his people to do: to leave the familiar and the comfortable, to embark on a journey full of threats and promises and, gripped by a vision of a world loved by its Creator, to risk everything in its pursuit. Never the romantic, Jesus of Nazareth followed suit by inviting people to follow him to the ends of their world, simply with the promise that even if it all ended in tears he would never desert them – that in leaving, journeying and, maybe, arriving, they would find that God is faithful and will love them beyond death itself.

Well, I'll go with that one. But do not, under any circumstances, try to get me on a cross-Channel ferry in winter ever again.

18

MOTHER TONGUES

If I asked you, 'Who are you?' how would you answer?

This is not an idle question, but it is not as easy to answer as it might at first seem. You could give me your name, or even tell me your life story. You could tell me about your family and what motivates you to live your life the way you do. You could tell me lots of things and yet, still, I would not be sure just *who* you are.

Identity matters. And when we are threatened or attacked it matters most urgently.

In Indonesia in the late 1990s, violence had brought to an end thirty-two years of corrupt rule by General Suharto and his family, but the brunt of this explosion of frustration and rage was borne by the ethnic Chinese community. Homes and businesses were mercilessly trashed. Men were summarily killed. Women were raped and abused. Even some of those involved were shocked by these appalling events, which saw generally placid Indonesians turn into vicious racist murderers overnight. But to be Chinese was simply to be isolated, afraid and demeaned.

The response of the Chinese community since the 1960s had been to find creative ways of maintaining their identity as Chinese people without creating a ghetto. And they tried, against the odds, to keep alive their mother tongue. In speaking their native language – despite the problems that could cause them – they could tell the stories of their people, acknowledge their roots and celebrate their uniqueness. And none of this detracts from their being Indonesian and 'seeking the welfare of the city', as the Old Testament prophet Jeremiah once put it.

These are not the first people to have faced questions of identity under powerful threat from others. The Jews of the Old Testament developed legal and religious mechanisms and taboos for maintaining the purity of their race. They were trying to ensure that future generations never forgot who they were, what their story was, and out of which rock they were hewn. Indeed, they could only live in the now if they knew where they had come from in the past. This distinctiveness is something for which they have had to pay very dearly in subsequent generations, the Holocaust being just one such example. The Palestinian people have fought and continue to fight a similar battle: how to maintain their identity as a people when they are denied dignity, place and a history.

It is not too great a leap of either reason or imagination to observe that the cited examples are mere illustrations of what it means for all of us human beings to survive and thrive. To be sure, race and mother tongue are not the only means of determining identity. But they help us realise that knowing who we are is a matter of great import. The novelist Laurens van der Post once said that if you don't have a story to tell, you don't have a life to live. In the West we have become so accustomed to living in the here and now, anxiously storing up treasures for the future, that we have lost our sense of identity, rooted in our past belonging. Learning stories and appropriating them takes time – but maybe there is no more important task for us. If we forget who we are, and simply identify ourselves by our differences from other people, we will imagine no coherent future.

It is not for nothing that God told the Israelites never to forget where they had come from: wandering tribes, made into a nation, liberated by God from oppression in Egypt, accompanied through the deserts, and delivered into a land of responsibility and nurture. Jesus broke bread and poured wine, telling his friends to do this together and remember him. This repeated action would always speak of sacrifice, love, grace. And, in speaking of violence redeemed, it might even give meaning and hope to suffering people, thus shaping how they in their turn treated others.

So, who are you?

19

ON THE MOVE

I hate having to admit this, but I am a slob. I know these things are relative, but if it's a choice between staying in the house and reading a book with music in the background or going for a walk round Tooting Common, I know which one I prefer. Walking is, for me, a matter of choice. Of course, I enjoy climbing mountains and walking the fells on holiday, but I can choose when I go walking, who I go with, how far I ramble, and I can change my mind at any point and go home. For millions of the world's people, however, walking is what they are condemned to do from the moment they are born.

One of the most emotive and repeated images to have assaulted us from our television screens in the last decade has been the long straggle of desperate refugees fleeing famine or war. Millions of people on the move from what was a home to an unknown destination and undesired fate. Anonymous and unwanted, they walk the earth in search of somewhere that might be called home, that might offer security and welcome, safety and warmth of society. And even if refugees have become a dehumanised touchstone by which comfortable Western politicians prove how 'tough' they are, nothing can take away the power of the images we have seen for ourselves. It could be you and it could be me one day.

Religious people – especially Christians like me – should be at the forefront of understanding the plight of refugees.

The earliest Jewish credal statement in the Old Testament begins: 'My father was a wandering Aramaean . . .' Abraham was called by God to pack up his stuff, leave the place where he was settled and go on a journey the destination of which was unknown. Moses was called to lead the people of Israel out of slavery, through forty years of homelessness in a desert. The people of God are always on the move, being called to travel light, not to be rooted to 'things'. They are beckoned to live and walk into an unknown future with only one certainty: that God who calls them will not desert them on the journey.

Clearly, going on a journey means leaving some things behind and joining with others – often others whom we might not have chosen for ourselves. But if God's calling to his people is for them to become mobile, travellers, refugees, homeless in the world while seeing the whole world as home, then these same people should be the first to recognise the real cost for the world's refugees and asylum-seekers.

It is surely timely for the Christian churches who recognise the plight of refugees and support those agencies which seek to alleviate suffering to examine again just how lightly to the world they are travelling; just how far the priority of God for the poor, the homeless and the unloved is reflected in their lives and structures. Or, to change the image again, to ask whether our discipleship of Jesus finds us wearing walking boots or carpet slippers.

20

THE CREDITABLE CARD

I've decided to invent something that will revolutionise the lives of millions of people. Like all inventions, it came to me by way of sheer inspiration and its beauty lies in its very simplicity. It is called *The Creditable Card.*

It's basically like a credit card, but it stops you buying things instantly and makes you wait. During the waiting time you will probably decide you didn't need whatever it was, anyway. The advertising slogan would be clever and accessible to all: 'Creditable Card: It puts the waiting into wanting!' There – that will upset the banks and finance companies!

Every child would be given one of these at the age of five and would be unable to buy anything (even via parents) without it. And in this easy, but effective way, we would educate an entire generation about values and priorities and time. In this way we would deal a hefty blow to the culture of consumer greed and instant gratification.

But our children will not find the experience of waiting any easier than we do. (An academic complained to me recently that even his university staff have not quite grasped that if he is sitting in his room reading a book, he is not simply doing nothing or just wasting time!) In the brave new world of modern communications we get bombarded by instant news from all over the world or even the universe. Advertising tempts, seduces and presses us to want and to want it now. In the age of the Internet we are in danger of confusing information with knowledge or – even worse – wisdom.

Yet there is wisdom in learning to wait. When the Israelites were delivered from exile and slavery in Egypt, they wandered for forty years in the desert. And during this time, as an Asian theologian, Kosuke Koyama, has suggested, they had to learn a vital lesson: human beings cannot live on bread alone, but need the word of God. In other words, we are not just materialists and consumers – even if the advertisers think of us in that way. Forty years to learn one lesson!

When I used to show local schoolchildren round the ancient church building where I was the vicar, they were invariably rushed. Like all children they didn't want to miss out on anything and tried to get the whole experience as quickly as possible – a bit like trying to understand art history by sprinting round the Louvre. Perhaps they didn't grasp the significance of the Saxon cross dating back to the 800s. Or the font which was sculpted during the reign of William the Conqueror. Or the inscribed list of Vicars of Rothley which go back to the year 1277. Or the desperately moving Elizabethan memorial to a dead wife by her young husband – she died aged thirty-two giving birth to her twelfth child (having already watched several of her children die in childhood).

Some good things in life cannot be learned except by taking time and waiting for understanding. So, is anybody out there prepared to give the Creditable Card a go?

21

IS GOD OVER HOBBIED?

I know a wonderful elderly man, now in his mid-nineties, whose wife once described him as 'over hobbied'. He married her late in life and she was staggered by the sheer range of his interests. He is a 'friend' of numerous English cathedrals, loves heraldry and water marks, and once showed me his compilation of the oldest firms of solicitors in Leicestershire. I took him on several occasions to visit cathedrals and abbeys. For him it was an interesting day out; for me, in contrast, it was an education. Apart from sport and pop music everything seems to interest him. He is infinitely curious about the world. His name is Ralph.

But, in one sense, his name could be God. You see, if you read or listen to the story of creation at the beginning of the Bible, God seems to be falling over himself to create variety and diversity. There's jungle and desert, ice floes and mountains. Trees compete for height and grandeur while flowers paint glorious collages of colour – often in places where life seems in short supply. There is rain and sunshine, snow and fog, oceans and puddles. And everything has its place and its purpose . . . apart from wasps, that is. And some things seem to have been created just for the fun of it. I read the creation narratives in Genesis and hear God laughing at the fun of creating a world that is alive and evolves in amazing ways, in one sense creating itself.

Now something has gone wrong with all this. I don't know many people who think of the creation story as being funny or full of fun. And this, I think, is tragic. Creation is the work of a God who loves and laughs it into being. He looks at each stage of his handiwork and says: 'That's brilliant!' You can almost hear him chuckling with the sheer playfulness of his own intentions. It's as if he loves it so much he keeps adding a bit more into the equation. For example, having created humanity, he thinks it would be great to step back and let Adam name the animals. 'You do this bit', he says, 'and you'd better enjoy it! Cos just when you think you've exhausted your dictionary of names, another little crawlie will turn up and you'll have to stretch your imagination even further!'

God comes over as being so playfully creative and curious that Ralph's wife might well have said that God, too, is over hobbied. To be curious about the creation is to enjoy its variety and to join in the creative fun of God himself. It means looking at the world, ourselves and God through a different lens. And it means being caught up in the endless playfulness of the creator. After all, if we are truly made in the image of this God, then we had better display some of the characteristics that are essential to him.

But if you ever let slip in Ralph's hearing that you are interested in Leicestershire solicitors, beware: there's a very, very long explanation about to follow!

TIMES OF LIFE

22

THE POTENTIAL OF A BABY

O K, get your hankies out – this one's a weepie.
I have three children, now aged fifteen, nineteen and twenty-one. I was at the birth of each of them and I shamelessly admit to having wept buckets as each one was delivered. They were all so different, so unique, so messy. And, boy, did they have well-developed lungs! When my youngest son was born in a hospital in Kendal I wrote this:

> God,
> creator of life,
> renewer of life,
> redeemer of life:
> you made us beautifully –
> like love incarnate.
> Your image, so easily to be spoiled,
> yet impossible to erase.
> And, in a small, ruddy face,
> with grasping hands and searching eyes,
> light explodes on an unsuspecting world
> and brings indescribable joy.
> It makes me weep for the wonder of it.
> It makes me laugh for the promise of it.
> It makes me long for heaven.

Now I recognise that I am no poet. But the sheer fantastic miracle of tiny human flesh and soul, held in my own hands, was too moving not to find some expression in words.

In that powerful moment, that realisation of the uniqueness of the life taken from the womb and placed in your hands, in that moment I was humbled, grateful, amazed. But I was also fearful. The future lies open before that child and I cannot control it. He will grow to laugh and cry, cut his knees and get dirty. He will start to question and develop his own mind. I will not be able to spare him the pain of life's journey, the agony of unrequited or lost love, the loss of what might have been had different choices been made.

And I wonder what Hitler's parents thought when they looked into the searching eyes of their son and wondered and wept? Or what hopes surrounded the birth of the peasant woman who became Mother Teresa of Calcutta? The Gospels tell us that the mother of Jesus took her baby to the Temple in Jerusalem only to be accosted by an old man who promised her that this harmless baby would one day break her heart. Having heard that, did Mary ever look into his eyes and hands and feet and fear for their wounding?

The miracle of new birth brings with it, inextricably and inevitably, the possibility of joy and pain. That is what it is to be human. That is what it means to be made in the image of the Creator.

23

DANIEL K.

W hat ever led our ancestors to name a place Lower Piddle? Or Upper Slaughter? Or Looe? (Of course, in the spirit of competitiveness, the French have to go one better and name their place Toulouse!)

I once found myself in an Austrian Volkswagen bus being driven from Linz to a small town in the north of Austria close to the border with Czechoslovakia (as it then was). There were eight of us in the bus, including two small children. As we passed a lovely lake surrounded by pine forests the peace was broken by the voice of the little four-year-old boy, Daniel K. He suddenly decided to ask his father what this particular lake was called. The reply was simple: 'It is called Lake Whateveritwas.' 'Why?' asked Daniel. 'Why what?' asked his Dad. 'Why is it called that?'

Now this presented a problem. The name was obscure and not descriptive of the place itself. Daniel's dad was doing his best, but it wasn't satisfying this four-year-old bag of curiosity. By the time Daniel had asked 'Why?' for the eighth time, his father was almost at breaking point and his mother said (in a this-is-the-last-word-on-the-matter sort of way): 'It just is! That's why!' Thus was Daniel's life preserved a little longer.

Now I am an adult I have enormous sympathy with Daniel. Surely it is a good thing to keep asking why things are the way they are. There is so much to discover about the world and why it is the way it is. For it is surely true that we can only truly appreciate the answers once we have identified the right questions. To keep on asking, as scientists must do, why things are as they are, is to be open to wonder. I think this is exactly what Jesus was getting at when he looked adults in the eye and told them they would have to become like children if they were to enter the kingdom of heaven: never lose your curiosity or the courage to question everything!

In a world of incredible busyness and activity, with wall-to-wall entertainment and floor-to-ceiling images, ear-to-ear noises and musak musak everywhere, it is difficult to pause for thought. The pace of life militates against us stopping long enough to recover the capacity simply to wonder.

And yet when I read the Psalms of the Old Testament I cannot get away from these ancient poets being moved and excited and challenged by what they could see of a wonderful and mysterious world. Their encounters with the living God caused them to fear and wonder. And they were provoked into asking questions about God, the world and themselves, even where the answers might potentially challenge their world-view right to its roots.

I don't think anything has changed. Where there is no wonder, no vision, the people perish. So I for one will keep asking 'why?' and 'when?' and 'how?' And, like Daniel K., I won't be satisfied with being fobbed off by people with no vision, no imagination, and no courage to ask the same questions.

24

TYING THE KNOT

❖

In my time I have conducted somewhere between 100 and 150 weddings. That's a lot of vows and a ton of confetti. So I think I've now earned the right to have a moan and get one or two things off my chest. Don't get me wrong: I love weddings, love getting to know the couples during the preparation, love the excitement and the colour, love the nervousness, and really love hearing the same three jokes in every best man's speech. (OK, the last one was a lie.) One of the best bits of being an Anglican vicar is getting to do loads of weddings.

But, the privilege is edged with responsibility, too. Read the bridal magazines (and I don't) and you get an idea of how much time, energy, thought and planning goes into the wedding day itself. Clothes, flowers, building, photographers, reception layout, seating plans, who can't sit next to whom because they no longer speak – all this and more besides. The average cost of a wedding in England now is between eight and ten thousand pounds. Then there's the stag night, hen night, presents for the bridesmaids, choosing rings, booking the honeymoon, and the list goes on.

Well, let me just put this question very simply: how much energy, time and thought goes into the marriage? Not the wedding and all that happens on the day, but the marriage? Surely the relationship itself deserves as much if not more investment than the planning of the day itself? In my last parish we invested a lot of time and imagination in preparing couples for their marriage together, not just the wedding day. We helped them think about how relationships work, how conflict can be understood and faced, how priorities are set and how feelings and emotions can be articulated. The response was almost universally effusive.

Now this might be contentious, but it seems to me that we live in a culture that sentimentalises love and reduces marriage to a contract. Most cards given to couples at their wedding will have on them somewhere a pink love heart. This is the icon of love which is found everywhere. But I would like to offer a different icon, a more realistic symbol which can become a lens through which we think about and see marriage or any other relationship: it's a cross. It speaks of a love which is self-sacrificial and vulnerable, a man with his arms open wide in welcome and embrace. It is totally realistic about the other person, harbouring no illusions and offering no pretentious self-images. It is a love that is costly and cannot hide, which faces the truth and therefore sets the lovers free never to have to hide.

I think that grasping this icon of love turns weddings into great celebrations. It is surely not coincidental that one of the most powerful images of heaven in the Bible is that of a wedding celebration. The first event in the public ministry of Jesus, according to John's Gospel, was when he went with his mates to a wedding and rescued the party by turning water into wine – the best quality wine at that!

(But perhaps you can explain to me why, when my wife called me a 'model husband' recently, I found the dictionary defining 'model' as 'a very small replica of the real thing'.)

25

WORSHIP AND WORK

One rainy day late in the summer, my wife and I went to visit Hampton Court Palace. We'd never been there before and thought we ought to see it as it's not far from where we live. Now I have to be honest: I hate doing the tourist thing and I hate being simply a voyeur of 'interesting artefacts'. The weather didn't help, being pretty awful all day. But, we went anyway and I was really glad we did. It's an amazing place, built originally in 1514 for Cardinal Thomas Wolsey. It was enlarged and embellished for King Henry VIII, who obviously didn't have an impoverished or ascetic view of life!

Anyway, the reason I'm telling you this is that I came across something that day that teased my imagination. The palace has a magnificent chapel and, when we went, it was full of groups of tourists who appeared to have different levels of interest in or comprehension of its magnificence. But the thing that caught my attention was the sign outside the chapel, just by the door through which you enter the place. It said: 'This is a working chapel.' I found myself wondering why it said 'working'. What was intended by this? Indeed, how does a chapel 'work'?!

The order or form of service which goes on in a church or chapel such as this is often referred to as 'liturgy'. This comes from a Greek word which means? Yes, you've guessed it, 'work'. In other words, worship is work. It demands something from the worshipper, expects a price to be paid for the experience. Worship, then, is not an easy activity designed for the convenience of consumers who want everything in life to be smooth and easily or instantly accessed.

Now, given that we live in a convenience culture in the West, you might be thinking that this is the final nail in the coffin of organised religion. But I think you would be wrong to do so. All this suggests is what every human being knows anyway: that is, that valuable things are costly. Worship of God, an encounter with the Creator, Sustainer, Lover and Healer of the world is not a thing to be treated loosely or lightly. An engagement in worship or reflection will come at personal cost and will demand that the worshipper be exposed, challenged and transformed by the experience.

Now I realise that this is not trendy stuff. A convenience society of powerful consumers is not patient with anything that makes you work or wait. Shouldn't religion be easy and accessible, we ask? Well, God is a realist and never sells people illusions. Jesus told his friends that if they wanted to follow him they would have to pick up a cross and carry it. In other words, it will cost you your life.

At Hampton Court Chapel we had a good wander round and enjoyed absorbing the atmosphere. But we were observers and it cost us nothing. Next time I go there I want to go deeper into the place's purpose over half a millennium. I want to go as a 'worker'. I want it to cost more than just an entrance fee.

NANTES TRIPTYCH

E ver since I overheard an American tourist in Paris
describe a Van Gogh masterpiece as 'kinda cute',
I've enjoyed spying on people in art galleries. Most
people go to a gallery to look at the exhibits. But me? No. I
go to watch the people looking at the paintings and sculptures.

One of the best places to go in London these days is Tate
Modern on the South Bank. You can have hours of endless
fun just watching people trying to make sense of what they
are looking at, wondering if the fire extinguisher on the
wall is an exhibit or . . . a real fire extinguisher. A year or
two ago I went down there on my day off. The place was
packed. Now, I usually avoid those little cubicles with videos
running in them, but this time I came across a large room
containing three huge video screens. It was called *Nantes
Triptych* and was created in 1992 by an American called Bill
Viola. Everybody should see this.

The left-hand screen shows a woman about to give birth.
We share the last thirty minutes of her labour and the birth
of her baby. The right-hand screen shows the last thirty
minutes of an elderly woman's life – in fact, it is the artist's
own mother. Between the two is a larger screen depicting
the dreamy mystery of life between its beginning and ending.
The loudspeakers pour out the sounds of the young woman's
expressions of pain and the aided breathing of the elderly
woman. Explosions of ethereal noise from the central screen

weave in and out of the other two. The effect is beautifully atmospheric, totally engaging and powerfully moving. The three screens run simultaneously, inviting the viewer to share the filmed experiences and contemplate the mystery of life from its beginning to its end.

So, why, I ask myself, did so many other people just wander in, watch a bit, then walk out again?

It seems to me that the traffic of people in and out of the room during that particular half hour said something about the sort of life we lead these days. Instead of staying with the film and the experience of it, people left and went in search of other stimulation. It is clearly too hard simply to sit or stand for thirty minutes in one place; they had to be seeing more things, getting more entertainment, moving on to something new.

But some experiences in life need to be lived with and through. As in the video, you can't rush birth. To watch the woman and her partner waiting for it to happen is not easy. You feel helpless just standing and watching. As the life of the older woman draws to a close, there is something unnerving about simply waiting and not being able to influence events. You know the inevitable is about to happen, but you can't do anything about it . . . except walk away, that is.

Perhaps we are just not very good any longer at stopping and staying still. Perhaps this sort of art gets too close for comfort, confronting the tourist with uncomfortable questions about the mystery and sacredness of life itself.

I stood mesmerised for thirty minutes. Then I went out and looked with a total lack of comprehension at a pile of bricks on the floor. I think I missed the point with that one.

MICHELANGELO'S ANGEL

I have to make a confession which, as someone who claims to be a sort of art lover, is somewhat embarrassing. I have never been to Rome. OK, it's not like admitting I've sent my children up the chimneys to earn some cash. But everybody tells me that I have JUST GOT TO see the Sistine Chapel ceiling and visit the galleries and . . . I suppose what they mean is, get some decent culture . . . 'live' as it were. I am told that the Tate Modern doesn't compare . . . but I think that's just snobbery.

Well, I would actually like to go to Rome some day just to see what Michelangelo got up to on that ceiling. He was clearly regarded as a genius in his own day and that judgement has grown ever since he died in 1564! (Coincidentally, but not importantly, he died exactly 390 years to the day that John Travolta was born in 1954. I think we should refrain from making obvious comparisons between the respective art of *Saturday Night Fever* and the Sistine Chapel ceiling and simply move swiftly on.)

There is a famous story about Michelangelo which appeals to me greatly. Apparently he was rolling a huge boulder down a hill, using all his strength to manoeuvre it. Someone stopped and questioned him about it, stating that it was just a huge piece of rock. Michelangelo replied that he was in a hurry because there was an angel waiting to get out of it.

Now I like this story because it demonstrates how one man can see something dead and not worth bothering with, while another man sees within it the potential for something beautiful to emerge. Michelangelo saw the perfect sculpture before his eyes; he simply had to chip away at the rock until the angel could be found within it. He looked more deeply, saw more clearly the potential before him, and committed his energies to creating a beauty which others could not at that point recognise or imagine.

You get a similar idea from the Creation stories in the Old Testament book of Genesis. God seems almost playful as he brings order out of the chaos of the world's first day. He sees the potential for life and beauty and fruitfulness and fertility. He imagines a complex world full of complex life and the possibility of love within and through it all. He sets the creation free to grow and burst with life and possibility. And, in so doing, he opens up the risk of that beauty being wrecked, disfigured or disregarded . . . a bit like Michelangelo sculpting his angel and then wondering what would happen to it at the hands of future generations.

But if I and you are made in the image of God, then this says something to us too. Do I see the potential and the hidden beauty within other people? Or do I simply see the hard and seemingly impenetrable surface rock and ignore it? All things considered, I think I want to look through Michelangelo's eyes and not those of the bystanders who simply watch and cannot see.

28

VITAL STATISTICS

I was sitting with my family round the table after our evening meal one day when my daughter, Melanie, asked me about the role of the generals in the First World War. Leaning over the plates and the oven gloves, she explained that she had an essay to write for her GCSE History course. Trying to be helpful I suggested she read some of the great First World War poets – Wilfred Owen, Rupert Brooke, Siegfried Sassoon – to get a feel for the futility of the trenches. My son, Richard, broke off from doing origami with the tablecloth and said there was no point in doing that because – and I quote – 'she won't get any extra marks for it'.

I thought education was about learning and growing and maturing and being curious. It seems, however, that today's educational culture is all about jumping through hoops to get the marks to get the qualifications to get to university to get the job to get the bank balance and the foreign holidays.

The *last* people to blame for this are the teachers. They are now required to concentrate on getting certain results so that the school appears well in the league tables. We also hear that they might be subjected to performance-related pay. What?! There are so many obvious questions about the statistics and pecentages-dominated education environment that it is difficult to know where to start.

This culture worries me. It seems that people and things are only valuable if you can measure them on a balance sheet or rank them in a league table. In a series of interviews in one of our national newspapers, famous people and their teachers talk about each other. Qualifications never get a mention. Inspiration, in contrast, does. But how do you measure inspiration and motivation given by a teacher to a child? How do you measure the growth in imagination in a child whose background militates against intellectual curiosity?

Isn't education meant to grow *people*, not simply put them through statistical sausage machines? As someone with five A levels and two degrees, I do realise that raising standards and broadening character are not alternatives, but belong together. But I do want to question this obsession with targets and tables which don't tell us a great deal about the *moral or character development* of our children.

I'm reminded of the Blind Willie Johnson song which says:

> I'm going to ask the question
> Please answer if you can
> Is there anybody's children can tell me
> What is the soul of a man?

He goes on:

> I saw a crowd stand talking
> I just came up in time
> Was teaching the lawyers and the doctors
> That a man ain't nothing but his mind.

Well, I believe a man is more than his mind. And he is certainly more than an object made to jump through hoops in order to be turned into a certain type of product at the end of the process.

It isn't just *how* we teach our children today that matters; it is *what sort* of children we are creating and what values they grow up with. I'm a worried man.

BEING
HUMAN

29

FEARFULLY AND WONDERFULLY MADE

I realise not everybody enjoys satire, but just listen to this. Jonathan Swift, writer of *Gulliver's Travels*, was so fed up with other people that he had the King of Brobdingnag describe human beings as 'the most pernicious race of odious little vermin that nature ever suffered to crawl upon the face of the earth'. Er . . . wow! He didn't mince his words did he? But before you take offence and turn away for fear of some tirade of personal abuse, let me explain why I felt the need to bring Swift's invective to your attention.

According to a survey reported in a national newspaper it was revealed that 63 per cent of horseriders prefer the company of their horse to that of their partner. Did you get that? Sixty-three per cent of riders prefer the company of their horse to that of their partner. Now, I don't know what their relationships with their partners were like – and I dread to imagine – but this epic bit of statistical trivia did set me wondering about how odd it is to be human in the first place. We are made to relate to others, yet as individuals we are so complicated. It's almost a miracle that any two human beings can ever get on in the first place. We human beings are such an enigma.

I mean, isn't it amazing that people who are capable of incredibly costly love can also commit appalling atrocities? Or that people who are clever enough to conduct intricate medical research can also create chemical weapons which will destroy people ever more horribly? It's a very peculiar business being human. And we are very complex creations.

Nearly three thousand years ago a poet found himself musing on similar themes. (I guess some things never change.) He wrote this of his own existence: 'I praise you, Lord, for I am fearfully and wonderfully made . . . My frame was not hidden from you, when I was being made in secret, intricately woven in the depths of the earth. Your eyes beheld my unformed substance.' The poem I am quoting from is called Psalm 139.

Sometimes I feel we ought to rephrase his assertion and say instead: 'I am fearfully and wonderfully weird.' Bruce Cockburn, the Canadian singer-songwriter referred to this as 'the burden of the angel/beast'. People are infinitely complicated beings and need to be respected as well as loved and forgiven. And this means that relationships between such people are going to be complex, too. I believe this should make us look at our relationships with awe and wonder, making time and effort to nurture them and learn how they work. It just seems incredible that you can get hours of advice on how to invest your money, but almost nothing if you want to get married. Isn't the relationship of the people more important than the building they happen to live in?

Well, I don't have a horse, so I don't have the problem of the 63 per cent. Anyway, once you've met my wife you'll realise that no horse would stand a chance!

30

WHAT'S IN A NAME?

❖

D o you ever wish your parents had given you a different name? You know what I mean, don't you? Some people bear the legacy of their parents' misspent youth or bizarre imagination. I once knew of a man called Randy Seaman: his parents obviously didn't see the potentially funny side of that combination.

Once I was given a paperweight for my desk as a birthday present. On it was written my name, Nicholas, and then the following: 'One who is always full of positive energy. Thinks winning thoughts. Has a lot of vitality.' What? 'Thinks winning thoughts!' I wonder if, having realised what the name actually means, my parents might now conclude they'd made a mistake. (What are 'winning thoughts', anyway?!)

What this illustrates, however, is that a name is more than just a title or a label. In Eastern cultures – including that of the Bible – a person's name includes their character, their very person. That's why when the Commandment says that we are not to take the name of God in vain, it is not about swearing, but abusing the very character or person of God or making a mockery of his nature by behaving in a way which denies him . . . which is far more serious, of course.

But this name business can get very interesting. For example, in the Old Testament there is a woman called Sarai whose name God changes to Sarah. Sarai means *barren*,

Sarah means *laughter*. The barren woman is transformed into one who laughs with joy and amazement at the friendship of God. And her name speaks of her very being and experience.

In the New Testament there is a woman who has been crippled for decades and has become an object of derision in her community. She is a non-person, of no value, who has no place in polite and pious society. Jesus touches her and calls her a 'daughter of Abraham'. In that one phrase he restores to her a unique dignity, gives her a place among her people, and allows her to stand tall. This case is typical of Jesus' gentle love of so many women who were regarded as being of no worth in the eyes of their contemporaries – especially those of the powerful men.

But these aren't freak or unique occurrences. For example, Jesus bears no illusions about the fickle character of his friend Simon; but he renames him Peter (literally, 'Rocky'!) and sees what this man might become in the future. I know that if I had been planning the building of the Church, I would not have gone for a character like Simon who regularly got the wrong end of the stick and led with his heart rather than his head. Fortunately, I am not Jesus.

I guess what is on my mind as I think about this is quite simple: does *my* name really say anything about me as a person? Or do I need to hear the name God gives me when he touches me and says he will love me to death? When people call me by name today, what will I hear: a label which traps me in a reputation or expectation I can't shake off? Or will I hear something else, the voice of God saying, 'You are made in my image and I love you'?

31

ALL WE LIKE SHEEP

Y ou don't need me to tell you that the media have
been dominated over the last couple of years with
the effects of terrorism, mass murder and the so-
called 'War against Terrorism'. Page after page of the newspapers has been filled with analysis, reportage, graphic
displays and comment on the serious issues in the world.
However, despite all the horrors of world affairs, I am relieved
that some other important stories still find space on the inside
pages. For example, I read a week or two ago that scientists
have demonstrated that . . . wait for it! . . . sheep can recognise
other sheep's faces.

Now this might not illuminate your day for you, but it
certainly arrested my attention. It had never occurred to me
to wonder whether or how a sheep would look at another
sheep, either with recognition or indifference. All the sheep
I have seen seem simply to keep their head down and eat the
grass. Not my idea of fun, but I'm not a sheep!

Now I've read the story in the paper, though, I've got
some real questions about these sheep. For instance, when
Billie the ram looks at Millie the ewe does he just see the
characteristics of the face and carry on chewing? Or does he
see a unique sheepy character and relate to her? Or – and
this is a tough one – does he get a window into her soul and
have a sort of emotional connection with her? Well, I don't
know the answers (and, if truth be told, I'm not terribly

interested to find out!). However, this line of rumination in my head has led me to reinterpret the language we often use to talk about sheep. 'All we like sheep have gone astray.' Here, to be like a sheep is to be a blind and stupid follower of other sheep. It is to be uncritical and unreflective. It is simply to conform.

But . . . if sheep do recognise each other, maybe we need to change our assumptions. 'All we like sheep need to examine how we look at other people.' What, for instance, do I see when I look at another person: my wife, the shop assistant, the street beggar, the friend . . . the enemy? What do I recognise in their face? Simply that I know them and whether or not to welcome or avoid them? A competitor for status or a weakness to exploit?

Way back in the Old Testament book of Genesis we read that God made people 'in his image'. So, when I look at another person, I am to see primarily a child of God, someone utterly unique. And, like me, this person is attractive and ugly, has successes and failures, strengths and weaknesses. This person is all sorts of things that either turn me on or off them. But, fundamentally, I am to recognise their inviolable value as a unique child of God, created in his image and loved to death by him.

So, there you go. All that from reading about an experiment with sheep. I can't wait till they get onto snakes.

32

HEROES AND HEROINES

Whenen I was a kid my heroes were all footballers. And they all played for Liverpool. At the moment they're generously letting the little clubs have a bit of success after having dominated domestic football for more than thirty years.

I remember once asking the children at a primary school assembly who they thought my heroes might be. They suggested Superman. Superman? A man who wants to save the world but can't even dress himself properly?! He wears his knickers outside his tights – how can you take *him* seriously?! The problem is, of course, that today we have no heroes. It sometimes seems that when anyone does something good or accomplishes some great feat we all start looking for the bad side of them, their inconsistencies, their feet of clay. We seem to love pulling them down and proving that they are just as feeble in some respects as the rest of us. Just look at the treatment meted out to President Clinton, Princess Diana or even Mother Teresa.

But it might surprise you to learn that the great heroes of the Bible, whose stories are recorded in gory detail, would never have been *got* by the tabloid press. Why not? Because they were perfect people? No! Precisely because they never once *pretended* to be perfect! They are depicted in all their fallen human glory, warts and all. They may have done heroic things, but they also had their dodgy sides. And neither they nor God were surprised by that.

One of my heroes is a dead German minister called Martin Niemöller. He was imprisoned by the Nazis in 1938 and spent over eight years in Sachsenhausen Concentration Camp. Released at the end of the Second World War he was hailed as a hero of the German resistance to Hitler. Yet the truth is that in 1931 and 1933 Niemöller strongly pressed people to vote *for* Adolf Hitler because he would be a strong leader who would restore dignity to Germany. As he witnessed the consequences of electing the tyrant, he changed his mind and suffered enormously for his courage. I may deplore his earlier blind patriotism, but I respect his willingness to pay the price of admitting he had been wrong and changing his mind – whatever the personal cost.

In the pages of the Bible we meet a succession of 'giants' (or, as the film title put it, *Angels with Dirty Faces*) whose stories are not told for their propaganda value. Moses is a murderer who, despite enormous strength of character, lets the Israelite side down on several notable occasions. David the great king of Israel commits adultery before effectively having the woman's husband murdered. Peter swears that he will protect Jesus to the bitter end . . . just before denying to a little girl in a garden that he even knew him. These heroes are to be examined in all their humanity and not sanitised to make religiously minded people happy with their fictional purity.

I think we all need heroes. But I also think we need to abandon our search for perfection in them. For me the greatest heroes are those who have no illusions about themselves, and have the guts to say 'I was wrong' and 'sorry'. They don't set themselves up as giants; they are only too aware of their human frailty. I want real heroes and heroines, people who own up to the real struggles and contradictions of life, people who don't represent unrealistic ideals, but are admirable because of their reality.

However, I wish Liverpool Football Club would ignore all this and win!

33

WORK AND FLU

I was sitting on the London Underground the other day minding my own business and trying to stay awake. But then I did the unthinkable and started reading the adverts above the seats opposite me. I decided after much careful thought that I wouldn't respond to the one that promised to increase my bust by two cup sizes. But it was the one next to it that caught my attention. It was for a drug and the caption said: 'Because deadlines don't care if you've got flu.'

Now, hang on a minute! If you've really got flu, you won't even be in the Tube reading the advert in the first place. If you've really got flu, you won't even be upright. You'll be in your bed wondering when you're finally going to die. It seems these days that people say they've got flu when they've only really got a bad cold or a bit of a chill. The real thing is devastating.

But what concerns me about the advert is not what it says about flu, but rather what it says about *us*. What sort of people are we who think that it is a virtue to ignore genuine illness and keep working. If you've got something nasty like flu, is it really responsible to go to work and share it with everybody else? If your body is telling you it needs to shut down, is it really noble or wise to play the hero or heroine and sacrifice all for the sake of keeping your employer happy? Is it really clever to assume that taking a tablet will make the illness go away, when you know that all it can do is mask the symptoms?

This seems to be a bit like a parable. It is easy to mask the discontent we experience with life, to try to escape from the effects of loneliness or disappointment by taking the drug of overactivity or excess busyness. But all we do is muck about with the symptoms without addressing the actual cause of the disease. It's a bit like taking aspirin to get rid of a headache caused by a brain tumour. I know this is stretching the idea here, but I am also reminded of the title of a book by an American cultural observer called Neil Postman: *Amusing Ourselves to Death*. By flogging ourselves in order to justify what we *do*, we are in danger of forgetting who we *are*.

I would hope that a good employer would value a sick employee enough to send him or her home to recover. I would hope that a good employee would value other colleagues enough not to inflict unnecessary infections on them. I would hope that whoever writes copy for stupid adverts would discover fairly soon that people are more than cogs in an economic machine, that people matter far more than the games they sometimes play in order to keep a job.

Work, surely, is meant to serve us, not vice versa. Or have I missed the point somewhere?

34

RIVERS OF TEARS

S everal years ago we were about to go on a long drive
to Austria to stay with friends there for a holiday.
Just before we went I bought the (then new) Eric
Clapton CD, *Pilgrim*. The first time I listened to it I nearly
cried. I put it on tape and listened to it again and again during
that holiday and the long drives across Europe until the tape
almost wore through. Among the riches on the album, there
is one song that stands out for me: 'River of Tears.' It is
beautiful, haunting, gut wrenching and unforgettable. Both
music and lyric evoke the sheer emptiness which only the
blues can express.

I don't know anyone other than Eric Clapton who could
make the guitar notes hang in the air longing for a response.
The whole song is stripped back and laid bare. The music
seems to hold great empty spaces which lesser musicians
would have stuffed with something electronic. But Clapton
makes us live with the emptiness, the experience of the river
of tears. And in doing so, he does us a huge service. He
won't allow us to run away from the loneliness and solitude
of this experience, or to fill it with noise. We are compelled
by both the beauty and terror of the longing to stay with him
and ache with a deep yearning for some hope.

Now, you might be thinking I'm being a bit morose and
miserable for my own good here. But, even if I don't happen
to feel particularly fed up today, many people will wake up

dreading what the day might hold for them. For most people their time will get filled with activity so there isn't the space to think or feel empty. But for others there will be no escape. And it's those who will identify with Clapton's song.

The great thing about blues songs like this one is that there is no cheap and easy resolution on offer. You don't get a verse popping up at the end in which everything suddenly gets sorted out. And I, for one, am glad! After all, this is what I am used to from the psalms of the Old Testament. There are people who think that the Bible in general, and the psalms in particular, offer trite and easy religious comfort to people in trouble. Rubbish! Read them for yourself and see what you find! Real poets describing real life, with no easy solutions to the dilemmas and experiences we all share by being human. No false but seductive illusions. No peddling of false hopes – even religious false hopes. No wishful thinking. The only thing the psalmists offer is that God, the Creator who loves his people, will not desert them. Nor will he exempt them from the realities of life and death, joy and suffering. The evidence of this is a man hanging on a cross, arms stretched out by nails, crying: 'This is how far I will go for you.' He doesn't even exempt himself!

Maybe the psalmists invented the blues without realising it. When they scream, 'How long, O Lord . . . ?' the river of tears is surely flowing. And Clapton dips into that river three thousand years later. And possibly might find the same echo in the air, the echo of God's whisper into the barrenness: 'I am here. And I will not leave you.' Even the river of tears eventually finds its way out to the open sea.

35

BEAUTIFUL DAY

Many of us were mightily relieved when, a couple of years ago, the world's greatest rock 'n' roll band, U2, put behind them the posturing of the 1990s and heralded a beautiful new dawn for good music. In fact, 'Beautiful Day' was the song that went to the top of the charts and made pop music seem redeemable after all – before becoming the theme music to ITV's football coverage. It's an original and powerful celebration of life and its richness. It basks in the warmth of the present and sees life as a gift to be enjoyed and lived.

OK, it's a great song and it would be easy to make too much of it. But the theme clearly strikes a chord with many of us – perhaps because a lot of us live today in the hope of a better tomorrow. We work hard today so that we can have time off tomorrow; but we work so hard that when tomorrow comes we are too tired to enjoy it. There is a real danger in our lifestyles that we miss the powerful reality and beauty of today because we are focused on what *might just come later*. 'Open your eyes!' beckons Bono, 'Look at the vibrant colours of today – because they will never be repeated.'

This song carries an invitation to be touched, taught and reached by other people, and this makes the difference between enjoying the present or fearing it. Jean-Paul Sartre once said: 'Hell is other people.' Well, he always was a miserable beggar and this is precisely what you might expect from a guy who writes a book called *Nausea*! But it is equally true that *heaven* is other people – or, rather, we glimpse it when we have the courage to open ourselves to the touch and reach of others. Simple human contact matters more than many of us realise.

I will never forget meeting an elderly woman in the Midlands and feeling her flinch when I took her hand in mine. My initial response was to wonder whether being touched by me was a deeply unpleasant and unwelcome experience. But it turned out that she had not been touched by another human being for a very long time. The absence of touch, even the touching of hands, must surely make for a sense of great isolation or lack of self-worth.

It is seriously significant that in the Gospels Jesus touched people whose society branded them worthless and dirty. He embraced the lepers who were avoided by normal people. He restored dignity to women whom men regarded as dirtied lesser mortals. The touch was as vital as the words he used.

What I constantly need to learn and relearn is this: touching others can be easy – allowing them to touch me is harder. Because being open to be touched by others demands humility, a dropping of defences, and a willingness not to hide behind image. And the day that happens is, indeed, a beautiful day.

RHYTHMS OF THE YEAR

36

LENT

I once went to a conference on a remote Scottish island. The journey up there from Bristol, in the aftermath of a night's violent storms, was awful beyond description. Half of Glasgow had an all-night party on the train and we missed every single connection. I felt sick and tired, and regretted having gone at all. By the time we got there I consoled myself with the thought that for the next week at least my mind would be engaged and my intellect stretched. I would face new theological challenges and have earnest discussions about God, life and the universe.

So you can imagine my horror when the conference leader introduced the first session with these words: 'You are all too good with words. So for the next two hours words are not allowed. Instead you will use pictures.' He then invited us to go off in small groups with a pair of scissors, a stick of glue, a large sheet of paper and a pile of colour magazines. We were instructed to draw a road on the paper. Then we were to stick on to it pictures from the magazines, thus depicting the journey of our lives. Yes, sticky pictures, glue and scissors! Oh great.

Now, I like to think I'm broad-minded and open to new experiences. But my first angry thought was, 'O wonderful! I've come all this way and paid all this money . . . to come to Playschool'. The only thing that could have made me feel worse was if someone had suggested we do . . . *roleplay*.

I reluctantly decided to join in. I began to find pictures that represented my life's key points and experiences and I stuck them on my paper. We were invited to draw a cross at any point on that road where we felt God had broken in. As I thought in the silence, and began to draw several crosses, I recognised in a simple way what words and theological argument could never have revealed so vividly: that God had broken into my life at all the points where I found life most hard and God seemed most distant. The empty places, where I could not escape my mortality, were the places of God's gentle presence. Stripped of the resources which I had learned to hide behind, I found myself to be loved by the God who had created me, loved me, and who had promised never to abandon me.

I might have been tempted to run away from the island. But, had I done so, I would have missed the experience of living with the emptiness and discovering in the desert place the presence of God. The experience was not comfortable, but nor was it unique. As a result of it I have had to learn to read my Bible differently, now noting how the experience of retreat into the desert is essential to God's people. From liberated Israelites spending forty years in the Sinai desert, through Israel in successive exiles from their own land and the securities of 'home', to Jesus being 'led by the Spirit' into the Judaean wilderness after his baptism so that he could be tested, the place of examination and withdrawal cannot be avoided. It seems always to be in the desert place, where all the extras are stripped away and we are left with nowhere to run to and nowhere to hide, that we discover the presence of God again.

If Lent is about anything, it is surely about this: that the discipline of the desert experience, while never welcome, is always fruitful. We simply need to stay with it and not be tempted to run away.

37

EASTER

On a trip to the Middle East in October 2002 I went with a group to visit some of the religious leaders in Jerusalem. Our schedule was tight and the time we were able to spend with each one was, therefore, limited. Their stories deserved more attention from us outsiders and it sometimes felt overwhelming just listening to fragments of stories of the immense suffering of different communities during the last century. Leaving one of these places we followed a narrow alley down a hill, escorted for our own protection by armed soldiers. The alley we walked down was the Via Dolorosa, the way of the cross, the road Jesus is reputed to have walked on his way to crucifixion. It was empty of people, a silent witness to the sad suffering of the Palestinian people held prisoner in their own home.

When Jesus walked that road he was not alone, but he too had an armed guard. Unlike us, however, his guards were charged simply with getting him in one piece to the place where he could be mercilessly tortured to death. Those who had promised to accompany him on this journey had, despite their bravado and good intentions, already deserted him, leaving him to face his fate alone. They, too, were subject to military occupation and knew how dangerous it was to offend the powers and authorities. Following the execution of their rabbi they hid in fear and wept for their now-collapsed world.

Now there are some people who want to jump straight from this to the resurrection a couple of days later. Somehow, they feel, all the pain and uncertainty can be avoided and we can focus on how previously fearful people became great and powerful evangelists and leaders. I have tried to find a delicate way to put this, but have failed: this view is dangerous rubbish.

With Jesus it is always the unlikely people who are honoured. In a patriarchal culture in which women have little value it is the women who stick with Jesus to his bitter end. It is the woman of dubious repute, Mary Magdalene, who is the first to encounter the risen Christ in the garden. And it is Peter, whose name might be translated 'Rocky', who, having let Jesus down the most, is gently restored. Walking on the beach – his place of work and the same place he had first met Jesus – he no longer has illusions about his own self-sufficiency and is able to love Jesus openly and without pretension or narcissism.

We would do well to avoid the temptation to jump from Good Friday to Easter Day. We must learn to live with the awful emptiness of Saturday before we can understand the confused joy of Sunday. And we will discover more of the power of this event if we stand with those who either followed Jesus all the way or who failed. If the Easter story says anything it demonstrates this simple truth: God is not surprised by our failures – but he is in the business of redeeming them. The price of this freedom is the sacrifice of our illusions about God, the world and ourselves.

And if that is true for individuals, it is surely also true for those broken communities in Jerusalem who long for Sunday's resurrection, but suffer still in Saturday's chasm.

38

PENTECOST SURPRISE

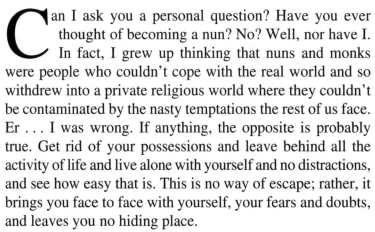

C an I ask you a personal question? Have you ever thought of becoming a nun? No? Well, nor have I. In fact, I grew up thinking that nuns and monks were people who couldn't cope with the real world and so withdrew into a private religious world where they couldn't be contaminated by the nasty temptations the rest of us face. Er ... I was wrong. If anything, the opposite is probably true. Get rid of your possessions and leave behind all the activity of life and live alone with yourself and no distractions, and see how easy that is. This is no way of escape; rather, it brings you face to face with yourself, your fears and doubts, and leaves you no hiding place.

Yet, paradoxically, many people are choosing to go on retreats these days. The retreat business is in great demand, perhaps because people feel trapped by the demands of contemporary life and long for peace and quiet and the feeding of the inner life, the spirit.

As a clergyman I have to say that I think the Church sometimes misses the point of its own major festivals. Or, at least, focus on one or two obvious points to the extent that other important stuff gets ignored or neglected. Pentecost is a good case in point. This is the day when we celebrate the coming of the Holy Spirit on the disciples of Jesus. After the crucifixion and resurrection Jesus' friends had gone into hiding. They retreated from the society which had murdered their friend and leader and tried to make sense of everything they had experienced. They needed this time to live with their memories and try to account for the amazing things they had witnessed. This couldn't be done in a quick coffee break between meetings. It needed time and space, together-ness and solitude.

When Pentecost came it was as if the whole picture made sense at last. They understood, the penny dropped, and they were, literally, fired up to live new lives with a new urgency and purpose. People who a few days and weeks before had been terrified for their lives now went out openly into the streets to speak of what had happened and explain what it all meant. But I wonder if all this could have happened had there not been a withdrawal first in order to give space and time to understanding what had happened to and around them. I suspect not.

So, I believe it is a mistake to jump onto the bravery of Peter and co. as they found new courage to preach the good news of Jesus on the streets before having lived with them in the upper room where they had first hidden then prayed. In other words, you can't have the open courage without having had the fearful and exposing hiding away.

It takes courage to retreat from a lifestyle of urgent and competing demands. It is not easy to draw a line and say, 'I am going away for a few days to be quiet – silent even'. It might sound to some people like the worst thing in the world they could ever do! But, it is worth it. Because it is in silence and solitude that the truth about 'me' can be found. It is here that no escape from the truth can be discovered. It is only by retreating, like a wise army, that we can regroup, learn lessons, and re-engage effectively in the world in which we live.

So, I join in the cry: 'Stop the world, I want to get off!' But only so I can get back on later, refocused and more alive than ever before.

39

HARVEST

S ome things stick in the memory like old chewing gum to the back of a chair. I remember as a child singing harvest hymns in school and church in Liverpool and wondering why we bothered. Come September/October we'd confidently sing, 'We plough the fields and scatter the good seed on the land'. Which was fine, I thought, except that we don't plough fields and scatter seed on the land. At least, not in Liverpool we didn't.

That's why I grew up feeling uneasy about singing such hymns. The connections between what I ate and the land that produced it were even then remote and tenuous. I had no idea where bananas came from other than the supermarket. In recent years our farmers have faced an unprecedented crisis in which higher food prices seem to deliver lower returns to those who produce it in the first place. Surely there's an irony in our singing harvest hymns and then going to the supermarket to pay as little as possible for our food, regardless of where it has come from and who has grown or produced it.

The other thing that bothers me is the nostalgia that seems to go with harvest time. We like the idea of farming the soil; but it is possible in today's world to live so remotely from the land that questions of food policy and growing processes are irrelevant to us. We are also enabled to live in a way that avoids being confronted by human mortality in the daily way that many of the food producers are. Life is fragile; we can have riches today and lose the lot tomorrow. Feast today, famine next week. If Harvest says anything to us, surely it points us back beyond the plastic covers of human cleverness to our dependence on God and our need for each other.

Recently a close friend of mine died of cancer. He was a remarkable man and is greatly missed. John was an energetic and visionary businessman, committed to charitable work and bringing the best out in people and communities. At his funeral I was able to claim for him a genuine integrity of life in which he held together two vital perspectives: first, that life is essentially a gift; and, second, that we have a moral responsibility to use our gifts and resources for the widest possible benefit. I think this fundamental attitude to life ties in well with harvest which is a festival, a celebration of the earth as a created gift from God, belonging to him and sustained by him. And we are stewards of this gift, called to be wise in its cultivation and just in its distribution.

In a cellophane-wrapped supermarket world harvest nudges us into a sometimes reluctant confession of greed, an admission that what we claim as a right is in fact a gift and a responsibility. If anything, harvest is the megaphone for the psalmist's great claim: 'The Earth is the Lord's and everything in it!'

And as I now go off to eat my cornflakes, I'd better at least read the packet and thank God for those who grew, harvested, packaged, transported and sold it to me. And I will thank God that it *is* cornflakes and not prunes that are set before me.

40

REMEMBER, REMEMBER

Nember is a funny month. You can't get away from being reminded to remember and not forget. First there's Bonfire Night, which is always good for a laugh despite the forgotten fact that it began as a celebration of the execution of a Roman Catholic by Protestants in England. Then comes Remembrance Day and all the battles that go with how it either should or shouldn't be observed. And both of these are preceded in the Christian calendar by All Saints Day when we remember those whom we love who have died. You can romanticise Easter and sentimentalise Christmas, but there's not a lot you can do to neutralise November.

But this does lead me to an important question. If you *lose* your memory, how do you know who you are? I have heard radio documentaries about people whose memories have been damaged or lost by illness and who no longer know who they are. Watch Arnold Schwarzenegger's film *Total Recall* and you are faced with this very question: what is the connection between memory and identity? The novelist Laurens van der Post made the same point when he commented that if you have no story to tell you have no life to live. Memory is vital to who we are; remembering where we have come from, then, is essential to understanding who we might become.

Some time ago I saw a documentary programme about a man, a professional musician, who had fallen victim to a nasty brain infection called viral encephalitis. Although he survived the illness, he lost almost all his memory. He can now remember only the last fifteen minutes or so. He has to live in a home. He spends his life writing down everything he does, everyone he sees, so that he can read his record of who he is. He has no idea of his own identity. He does not recognise his wife and family. He does not know who he is, where he is, or anything about his life thus far. His story is tragic.

Perhaps this is why if Remembrance Day did not exist, we would have to invent it – or, at least, something similar. For, if we do not recognise where we have come from, we cannot know why we are the way we are. And this applies to individuals, families and communities as well as countries. Indeed, someone once said to me that the problem in Northern Ireland or the Middle East is not that people have too little memory, but that people remember too much. But the truth is that all remembering is selective and reinforces the story we wish to believe about ourselves and our heritage – especially where we have been hurt.

But we cannot run away from the responsibility of what to do with our memories. It must surely be a great hypocrisy to observe two minutes' silence if my own life and relationships are characterised by the anger, selfishness or greed which, in the case of whole countries, lead to conflict. Jesus warned his friends that if they pray for God's kingdom of justice to come, they must begin by inviting God to change them first. Justice and peace begin with me, not the government.

Remembrance Day calls us back to remember where we have come from. It calls us back to an honest facing up to human greed and our lust for power and security. It calls us to refuse any selective remembering or romanticising of our history. Perhaps I can put it this way: each of us must choose either the way of justice and peace, or we are left with just ice and a community in pieces. The choice is ours. Remember?

41

CHRISTMAS CAROLS

Angels from the realms of glory

They appear on Christmas cards in the most bizarre places. They get confused with fairies. Even Robbie Williams got carried away and got to number one with a song about them. And you can bet your Christmas pudding on it: if there's a Christmas tree to be seen, there's one stuck indelicately on top of it. They are angels.

Now I would hazard a guess that if you go into the pub and announce to the people in the bar that you've just had an encounter with one, either the pub will empty *tout de suite* or you'll be swiftly removed from the premises. Mention angels and you're immediately consigned to loony-land where all sorts of imaginary friends can be conjured up.

So, what are we supposed to do with the Christmas story in which angels keep popping up? Are we to tell ourselves that it's nice for the little children to have a bit of magic? Or should we just feel a little bit embarrassed – like we do when someone reminds us that we once wore flares and thought The Osmonds were fab?

Well, I think we ought to be bolder than this. We should ask ourselves what part these funny creatures play in the stories of Christmas which we read in the Gospels. After all, these angelic beings are not simply wimps in white nighties, floating above the earth encouraging us to be nice to each other. No. They actually do embarrassing things. They appear before a soon-to-be-pregnant teenage girl and give her what most of us would regard as unwelcome – even bad – news. And just in case she is tempted to pretend nothing has happened, they even confront her fiancé and rub the bad news in. Later they interrupt the ordinary routine of a night's work for shepherds in the hills and invite them to come down from the hill to have their understanding of the world turned upside down in the presence of a baby.

I also find it quite funny that instead of charming the cultured people of the day, God sends the best, most out-of-this-world *choir* not to the Friends of the Jerusalem Philharmonic Orchestra but to these specimens of uncultured and unwashed humanity.

And that's the surprising place of angels in the Christmas story. They bring disturbing news to settled people. They roll back the curtain of the real world and open the eyes of working men to a vision of heaven. And they noisily and untidily bring good news to people who are willing to get off their backside and come down the hill to a stable. The bad news of today's experience will soon and unexpectedly give birth to good news for the world. That's all. Angels just bring the news, open our eyes, have a party and clear off again, leaving us to work out where we go from here.

Now. Try telling it like that in the pub . . . and watch the fairy fall off the Christmas tree with fright!

While shepherds watched

I don't know about you, but sheep don't grab me. They bleat, grow woolly and leave olive-like droppings all over the hillsides in the Lake District. They may be cuddly when made of soft fabric and stuffed with cotton wool, but they don't appeal to me as pets or objects of affection.

I know this might enrage some people who know better than I do, but looking after them can't be that exciting. Can it? I don't know what shepherds do all the time. And before all the sheep-loving early risers in Britain accuse me of outrageous slander, I admit my ignorance and scandalous lack of interest in sheep.

So, why am I talking about them now? Well, simply because they figure in the Christmas story which is being rehearsed all over the country during this month. Any child who doesn't get a major role in the Primary School Nativity Play gets a bit-part as a sheep, stood over by a shepherd who looks coy and uncertain. And here I must confess to being worried. Nativity plays and kiddies' Christmas story books sanitise the Christmas story and clean it up. It becomes an anodyne tale of bland people with towels on their heads who, devoid of any personality, stand around looking unimpressed by extravagant visions and the breaking in of God.

It was always the shepherds who grabbed me. There they are, sitting on the hillside minding their own business, enjoying or enduring a hard-working life and few exciting life expectations. They are viewed by the more respectable society people as dirty, servant-class, rude and graceless proles. And yet the ordinary routine of a night's work for these shepherds in the hills is disturbed by a God of surprises. And these working men find their ordinary working lives interrupted in the most unexpected way.

For a start, if God is going to do anything remarkable, or say something profound, he's going to do it to priests and holy people, isn't he? At least, that's what these shepherds would have believed. God is interested in people who are inside the holy club of people who 'do it right'. But that is where God the Creator shines a fresh and refreshing light on his own nature and way of working: he sends a massive choir of partying angels to invite – of all people – these guys to be the first to see the baby who would transform the world.

These are social outsiders, people with no pretensions and even fewer expectations of God encountering them in their everyday experience. Yet God opens their eyes to a new reality, a new perspective on the world, and invites them to leave the place of their old limitations and walk down the hill to a stable.

Now, maybe it's not stretching the imagination too far to suggest that if God, at that most pivotal moment in history, bothers first with these shepherds, he might just bother with you and me. Not because we are holy or have gained enough brownie points, but simply because he takes us more seriously than we take ourselves . . . and loves us more than we love ourselves.

If it comes to a choice between the priests and the shepherds, the holy or the great unwashed, the fundamentalists or the surprised . . . I'm with the shepherds. Despite the sheep and their peculiar habits.

In the bleak midwinter

Hasn't it been miserable enough already? We've had storms and winds. Half the country has experienced what one tabloid intelligently called 'floody hell'. And now Christmas comes and we sit around singing about bleak midwinters. It's enough to make you depressed.

I've always struggled with 'In the bleak midwinter'. Even as a child I had a sneaky suspicion that the hymn writer had lost the plot and thought Jesus was born on the Yorkshire Moors in a January blizzard. Was it really winter in Bethlehem? Did it really snow on snow on snow? Was the earth as hard as iron? Or was it just an ordinary Middle Eastern night with not a lot happening except angels breaking through the sky and singing? Didn't they worry about waking the children and getting complaints in the local papers?

I do remember, however, what the experience of a 'bleak midwinter' is all about. I don't mean the weather outside, but my feelings and experience inside. I was a curate in Kendal in the Lake District on the night when a plane was bombed out of the sky above Lockerbie. To relate the experience of that to the story of Christmas a day or two later was challenging. Several years later, and now vicar of a parish in Leicestershire, I went to the hospital to visit a family who were praying for the life of their husband and father in Intensive Care. He had been hit by a car and hope of recovery ebbed and flowed. The next day, Christmas Eve, his son came to Midnight Communion in church where I was preaching at a candle-lit service about the reality of Christmas. His father died on Christmas morning.

In these bleak midwinters of life's experiences, where the ground is hard and cold and comfort is not easily found, Christmas can seem like fluffy, trivial escapism. It can become unbearably romantic and cause a sense of yawning and fearful emptiness. The bland muzak in the shops, the fir trees that drop their deadened needles as soon as we decorate them with tinsel and chocolate, even the carols and drunken parties easily reinforce to the grieved and grieving just how fickle our lives are. Christmas might be special for the comfortable or those who wish to escape from reality. But to those who are in the bleak midwinter it offers no refuge.

So, I think it is brilliant that Christmas is about God's surprise. It speaks of God coming among us, right where we are, where the pain is most acute and the fear most dreadful. In the baby of Bethlehem – whatever the weather was like there at the time – we see the vulnerable face of a God who risks everything for us. This baby's hands and feet will one day be wounded grievously. And yet, even then, after the world has done its worst to him, he will still, three days later, open those hands in embrace and shine resurrection over the manger of Christmas and the cross of Easter.

There is nothing romantic in this. Just hope. And brute realism. And God among us.

Silent night

Who are they trying to kid? Do they really expect us to believe the stuff of Christmas carols? Really?

I mean, 'Silent night, holy night'? In Israel?! Why do we seem to want to believe that the night of Jesus' birth was quiet or especially holy? I think there's something going on here. I suspect a subtle plot, a cunning plan of Baldrickian proportions, by the carol writers to make us so romantic and comfortable with the Christmas story that we'll miss the point of it all. 'Silent night, holy night, all was calm, all was bright.' Er . . . was it?

I have to be honest about this. I have a problem with 'Away in a manger' too. 'The little Lord Jesus no crying he makes.' What?!? A baby that doesn't cry? That's new. That's a pretty incredible miracle, if you ask me!

Yet, perhaps the writers were on to something. Perhaps they were trying to say not that the Christmas story is un-believable, but that the miracle of God's coming among us was unexpectedly feeble. I mean, put it like this: if I were God and decided to enter the world I had created, to then live among these violent and greedy creatures called humanity, I would arrive on Planet Earth with the biggest noise ever heard. The trumpets would blaze, the heavens would open, the business of the world would come to a frightened full stop, and there would be absolutely no mistake about who is boss. I would stand on my status and I would demonstrate a bit of power and might. Thunder bolts would be in huge supply.

But what does God do? He comes as one of us, in the same way we come into the world. He is born as a baby at a time of astronomical infant mortality rates, in an obscure part of an occupied minor region of the Roman Empire. He subjects himself to disease, accident, oppression and injustice. One day the wood of the manger would be swapped for the wood of the gallows. His young, already widowed mother would watch her son's execution, her agonised love penetrating her own heart like a sword.

Bruce Cockburn put it like this:

> Like a stone on the surface of a still river,
> Driving the ripples on for ever,
> Redemption rips through the surface of time
> In the cry of a tiny babe.

God breaks into a lonely and wondering world. But he does so almost incognito. He puts himself where we are and makes himself vulnerable to all that our lives can throw at him. No shouting or banging the drum. No clinging to 'rights' or power. Just, in the still of the night, he is born of a young girl into a wonderful and yet fearful world. And in so doing he whispers into the silence: 'Now you know I am for you; I am on your side.'

Maybe I need the silence of a night to comprehend the power of *that* silent night.

O come, all ye faithful

'O come, all ye faithful, joyful and triumphant, come ye, O come ye to Bethlehem.' Er, no thank you – I don't think I'll bother. Bethlehem? Who'd want to go there? It's in the middle of nowhere and it's now a battle ground between Palestinian and Jew in their godless conflict. You can keep Bethlehem; I'll stick with where I am.

Well . . . This is missing the point somewhat. The call to go to Bethlehem is really getting at something rather different from this. It seems to be a call to be surprised by God in a surprising place. It is a habit of God to do this. In the Bible he keeps upsetting people by intruding where he is not welcome (like in the corridors of power of the Roman Empire – which, incidentally, is not the name of an Italian cinema). In the Gospels Jesus keeps talking to the wrong people: collaborators, sick and infectious people, prostitutes and fat cats. He seems to be embarrassingly indiscriminate in who he hangs around with. He touches people who should not be approached and listens to people whose story has been untold for a generation.

And I guess that's where I begin to struggle with this particular carol. Who are 'the faithful' who are encouraged to visit Bethlehem? And why are they singled out for special invitation? When I read the story of that first Christmas in the Gospels I find God inviting outcast shepherds to go walkabout in work time and foreigners to bring symbolic gifts to a strange family. It is rather faith-less people who are beckoned and welcomed.

Now, don't get me wrong. I'm not suggesting for one minute that Christians are not invited to celebrate Christmas! Rather, I'm suggesting that we ought to widen the field a bit and invite the unfaithful to come to Bethlehem to gatecrash a party they didn't know was happening. They might spend the whole time wondering whose party it is; but they'll probably find out before they leave. And they might be surprised to find how welcome they are, even if they feel their credentials are inadequate. The God of the Christmas story has a habit of loving surprises, springing jokes, inviting anyone who will come to join him where he is.

Bethlehem might not be the most attractive place to visit. It's a stable which frames this particular tableau. It has real dirt, real smells, real people, real bewilderment and real uncertainty. There is no promise of an easy or a healthy life. There is no guarantee of a comfortable lifestyle. There is no security and no fully comprehensive insurance protection. Indeed, the host of this basic accommodation will one day find hospitality in short supply and find his joyfulness and faithfulness getting him nailed to a cross.

But, whether I consider myself to be faithful or faithless, he looks me in the eye and invites me to prepare for Christmas, to celebrate God among us. So, come all ye people, ye who are curious about what is really going on at Christmas, come to Bethlehem. And be surprised.

And . . . er . . . rewrite the carol . . .

HAPPY NEW YEAR

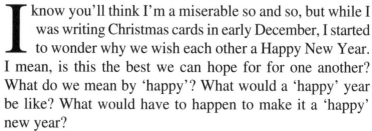

I know you'll think I'm a miserable so and so, but while I was writing Christmas cards in early December, I started to wonder why we wish each other a Happy New Year. I mean, is this the best we can hope for for one another? What do we mean by 'happy'? What would a 'happy' year be like? What would have to happen to make it a 'happy' new year?

The American Constitution declares without a hint of irony that all people have the right to the pursuit of happiness. But nowhere does it define what happiness is, nor how you would know when you had achieved it. Now, call me a party-pooper, but I don't think happiness is enough. I don't think it is the best to wish for someone. My personal happiness is not the greatest good, and the pursuit of it does not justify any selfish behaviour on my part. Happiness is great if you get it, but there is more to life than just a nice feeling of satisfaction. Martin Luther King said, 'A man does not a have anything to live for until he has found something worth dying for.' And dying does not usually figure in most people's top ten list of things that make you happy.

The vast bulk of people who have graced this earth during the last century or so have experienced cruelty, loss, war, poverty, debt, disease and worse. But, within those experiences many have also found fulfilment, purpose and hope. Within circumstances which appear to guarantee unhappiness they have experienced life in a different dimension.

Our calendar is dated from a man who not only gives shape to our calendar, but also meaning to our lives. Jesus Christ offered 'life in all its fulness'. But he never ever seduced people with illusions of happiness. Rather, he promised them that if they chose to go with him they would probably face a cross. For him and his friends there were more important things in life than mere happiness: faithfulness, for example, and costly love. He never romanticised or encouraged anyone to live with illusions about themselves or the world. And, echoing the harmony of death and resurrection, he has not changed his tune in two thousand years.

So, as the old year closes and the future opens up, beckoning in a new opportunity for all of us, we can join together in making a new resolution in the name of that same Christ:

> Let there be
> respect for the earth
> peace for its people
> love in our lives
> delight in the good
> forgiveness for past wrongs
> and from now on a new start.

May I wish you more than a happy new year!